CO-AJX-741

Community Power and Policy Outputs

A Review of Urban Research

Terry Nichols Clark

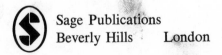

Sage Publications
Beverly Hills   London

For Susan Nichols Pulsifer
and her Witch's Breed

Copyright © 1973 by Terry Nichols Clark

All rights reserved. No part of this book may be reproduced or utilized in any form or by any means, electronic or mechanical, including photocopying, recording, or by any information storage and retrieval system, without permission in writing from the publisher.

For information address:

Sage Publications, Inc.
275 South Beverly Drive
Beverly Hills
California 90212

Sage Publications Ltd.
St. George's House
44 Hatton Garden
London ECIN 8ER

Printed in the United States of America

International Standard Book Number 0–8039–0343–X (C)
0–8039–03448 (P)

Library of Congress Catalog Card Number 73–90036

First printing

Contents

Figures

Tables

Preface

This brief volume grew out of a project undertaken for the Committee on Community Research of the International Sociological Association. It led to a Trend Report and Bibliography, which appeared in the UNESCO Current Sociology series. (The References at the end of the present book are based on that volume.) But a critique and synthesis of at least elements of research on community power, local governmental organization, municipal budgeting, policy outputs, and related matters promised to be of wider interest. Hence the preparation of this paperback. If readers from the curious undergraduate to the professional social scientist or city official seeking a compact review can find something of use, *Community Power and Policy Outputs* will have served its purpose.

Research on urban political phenomena has been changing rapidly; hence little attention has been given to works more than a decade old, except for a few classics, and many studies discussed are still in progress. I hope that a taste of the challenges and excitement facing the researcher dealing with these issues can be acquired from the following pages.

Most of the book was written while I was on leave from the University of Chicago, as Visiting Associate

Professor, Departments of Political Science and Sociology, and Institution for Social and Policy Studies,
Yale University, and at the Sorbonne (University of
Paris V). Financial support was generously provided
by the Institution for Social and Policy Studies at
Yale and the National Science Foundation (GS–
1904, GS–3162). This is research report No. 46
of the Comparative Study of Community Decision-
Making.

November 1973   T<small>ERRY</small> N<small>ICHOLS</small> C<small>LARK</small>

Introduction

Studies of community power and decision making are losing their distinctiveness. This is to be applauded, for contributions from this area can sharpen and enrich adjoining analyses. On the other hand, work on power and decision making alone, as we argue below, is enhanced in meaning if considered in a more general framework. A good deal of research in the last decade has helped fill in elements of such a framework. The community as a research site is losing its autonomy from the national system. Community characteristics are being isolated, and their impact on decisions analyzed. Values of citizens and leaders are increasingly investigated and compared. Centralization and decentralization are being related to community characteristics and to policy outputs. Several more general theories of power and collective decision making are taking shape; their linkage with community research both extends more general theories and provides them with more precise empirical content.

It is convenient to review research developments in terms of the framework presented in figure 1. Indicating the basic variables in analyses of community power and decision making, the figure also suggests some of the more important causal relationships. In the remarks which follow, we consider the variables presented, in numerical order, grouping certain variables for discussion.

Figure 1. Ten Fundamental Sets of Variables in Community Decision Making

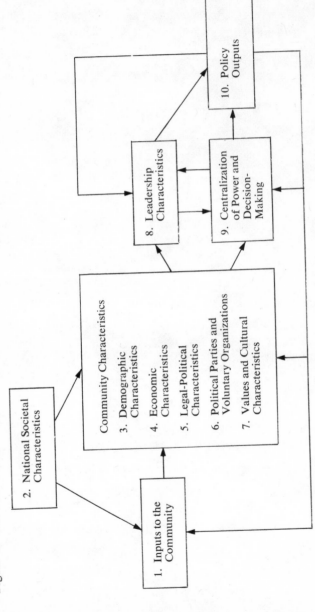

1 Inputs and National Societal Characteristics: The Issue of Local Autonomy

Community studies have too often assumed the community to be a closed system. Doubtless the empirical inexactitude of this assumption was long evident but, like basic assumptions in other areas, it vastly facilitated research. Even anthropologists' studies of communities of reasonably isolated peoples have acknowledged relations with the larger national society. Few have been so conscientious as Claude Lévi-Strauss in *Tristes tropiques*, pushing far into the jungles of Brazil searching for the unadulterated community of isolated villagers. But if most researchers have been less insistent on empirically autonomous communities, they have normally dealt only rapidly with the converse problem. That is, given that no community is autonomous, how is one to describe and analyze interdependencies between a community and the broader society of which it is a part? We have unfortunately little to go on in this area. But in contrast to a decade or so ago, the problem has become recognized as fundamental, and efforts are underway to provide answers. Let us review rapidly some of the kinds of answers emerging.

Linkage of the local community to the national society was always explicit for those who looked at the community largely from above. This was espe-

cially the case for traditional work in public administration, which inevitably dealt with the community
level but normally viewed functionaries at that level
as implanting administrative imperatives from above.
In France, where the idea of local autonomy is only
semi-legitimate, the field of local politics is treated in
most textbooks and basic courses as *l'administration
locale*. Public administration is complemented by
public finance, which has also long dealt with sub-
national fiscal matters. But for many years statistical
data were often collected and analyzed by lumping
together all governmental units below the national
level. Thus one finds a substantial literature on the
"determinants" of "state-local expenditures" report-
ing some of the stronger associations between expenditures and other state and local variables. In more
recent years, however, as efforts have increased to
isolate specific causal mechanisms associated with
different expenditure levels, one finds more often distinct studies of state activities on the one hand and
local activities on the other.

It is not our charge to review or criticize literatures
on public administration or public finance. We point
out simply that as students of communities incorporate in their analytical frameworks relationships to
the national society, they inevitably must draw on
related intellectual traditions.

The need to move in this direction is becoming
explicit in recent work. Vidich and Benseman (3–122
under References below), for example, dealing with
a single small town, focused explicitly on its linkages
with the broader society. Especially important medi-
ators, they found, were individuals combining the
roles of administrators and professionals—public

health officials, welfare officials, etc. In bringing new federal and state programs to the local level, they made the residents aware of their linkages with the rest of the society and generally channeled national orientations and value patterns. The same basic finding has been reported in other national contexts.

More often, however, community studies in the United States have portrayed local actors adapting legal and fiscal resources of higher levels of government to their own needs. Thus in *Who Governs?* Robert Dahl (3–59) analyzed how an aggressive mayor and urban renewal director in New Haven obtained massive federal funding with minimal local contributions. Similarly Edward Banfield in *Political Influence* (3–47) showed how Chicago *Tribune* representatives, with other Chicago actors, obtained legal support in the state legislature for an exhibition hall for the City of Chicago. If these two landmarks in the case study literature had been completed a decade later, it is likely that relations with higher levels of government, and some involving influence from above, would have been more prominent.

Indeed, the decade of the 1960s witnessed a dramatic expansion in federal programs concerning American cities. The best known in earlier years were public housing, highways, and urban renewal. To these were added the New Frontier and Great Society programs of the Kennedy and Johnson years, with their ambitious titles. Manpower and community organization programs under the Office of Economic Opportunity were often the most controversial, especially the Community Action Projects. Several other programs followed rather similar lines: Model Cities (omnibus agencies coordinating programs in poor neighborhoods), Judicare (legal assistance for the poor), and various public health, welfare, and manpower training programs. Established with primarily federal funds in the mid-1960s, these were often operated by social workers and community organizers with far more radical views than elected officials (and probably most citizens) in the same cities. To date we have only very partial accounts of how these agencies were established at all. Endowed (at least in the C.A.P.'s) with a mandate to encourage "maximum feasible participation" by the poor, by acting out this mandate the programs generated great controversy, and in the early 1970s they were drastically curtailed or abolished. Their major successor, in the U.S., is a program of "revenue sharing" whereby unitemized block grants by the federal government are made to state and local governments.

This diversity and change in programs provides the researcher with a remarkable spectrum of national-local linkages. A few general works have described the principal dimensions of these programs, such as those by Sundquist (1–166) and Moynihan (1–155). Hearings of various federal commissions have generated an abundance of documentation, especially for antipoverty and housing activities. There are also many, many evaluations of individual federally supported programs (3–37). Most evaluations remain unpublished or available only in limited number, although some of the more serious efforts are moving toward publication, such as a massive study by Roland Warren and his colleagues.

Researchers outside the U.S. have been conscious of the national dimension of community affairs from an earlier date. Just a few examples in the References are 1–133, 158, 174, and 4–64. How to deal analytically with the phenomenon of national-local linkages, however, remains unresolved. Clearly, case study materials are essential to chart the terrain. These remain few in number, and more are doubtless needed. One can employ, in a case study, various standard measures (reputational, decisional, etc.) for isolating the relative importance of local versus national or other nonlocal actors. A few studies, especially in France, have also begun to develop the idea of a *réseau*, which might be translated as social network or linkage pattern, joining local and national actors. In French communes the mayor, prefect, and other regional officials like the Inspecteur des Ponts et Chaussées often spend considerable time developing networks of contacts linking their constituency with the major agencies (especially in Paris) involved in decisions affecting the local constituency. Networks vary considerably, in good part as a function of the resources available to the local actor. Actors relying on ideological ties, such as a Communist mayor, may work primarily through their party structure and representatives in the National Assembly. A bridge inspector may develop contacts initially in his area of expertise, and then extend these to other ministries. We still need a more adequate typology of networks and efforts to explain their nature, intensity, and effectiveness.

The importance of such national-local relations seems to become more salient to researchers working in a new national context; the unchanging elements which most others take for granted become more clearly variables. Here one can mention the early but very perspicacious report on American national-local linkages by Charles Roig (1–158), and the recent effort by Mark Kesselman and Donald Rosenthal (4–10) to fuse certain concerns of national and local comparative politics. An impressive thesis by Jeanette Becquart-Leclercq documents the impact of the *réseau* on local policy outputs (school buildings, streets, etc.) in a sample of French towns (4–17).

It seems important to conceptualize the degree of local autonomy as one variable in need of measurement and analysis which together with others helps explain the operation of local affairs, as suggested in figure 1. A few propositions are available to this end. Roland Warren (3–38, 1–170) and then John Walton (1–169) developed the useful ideas of horizontal and vertical linkages across communities. Walton suggested that a consequence of increasing such linkages was greater decentralization of decision making. His reanalysis of case studies (1–169) tended to support this proposition. A recent work by Clark (1–123) isolates some forty-eight propositions linking national structures, legal patterns, local social and economic resources, and cultural ties to the degree of local community autonomy. Support for several propositions was found in analyzing data from fifty-one American cities, but clearly more careful empirical work is needed. Robert Alford has one international project underway in the area. A major problem here is the difficulty of operationalizing local autonomy. Several efforts have been made to reanalyze budget data for these purposes, such as computing the proportion of the local budget from higher levels of government. A more sophisticated approach is that of Ostrowski and Teune (2–11a), who suggest analyzing the degree to which expenditure patterns covary statistically with social and political characteristics of local, regional, or national levels.

2 Community Characteristics

Until the mid-1960s, most studies of community power and decision making were case studies of single towns. Correspondingly, researchers seldom allocated much attention to community characteristics differentiating their research site from others. In one of the most scrupulous studies, Dahl's *Who Governs?*, an appendix compared the position of New Haven with all American cities on many census-type variables. The purpose of this exercise, nevertheless, was not to analyze such variables per se but to suggest that New Haven was sufficiently similar to other American cities that the results could be legitimately generalized. However much subsequent researchers built on Dahl's results, in this respect they did not. Indeed, a major thrust of research in the late 1960s involved the explicit isolation of community characteristics which generated variations in decision making patterns. One way of summarizing this emphasis is to say that, in contrast to Hunter, Dahl, and most case studies concerned primarily with the question of who governs —the nature of power and leadership patterns in an individual city—subsequent comparative studies have tended to ask: Who governs, where, when, and with what effects? What are the specific characteristics of communities likely to encourage different patterns of

13

power and leadership, and what consequences emerge in specific policy outputs? See 4–4 and 3–1 for two collections of papers devoted largely to these questions. Before considering specific answers, we review briefly some major approaches to isolating community dimensions since these may be adapted to such questions as: Where, when, and with what effects?

In the same years that most case studies of community decision making implicitly assumed that communities were basically alike, other researchers were refining methods of differentiating between communities. Probably the most important tradition has differentiated communities according to the "functions" which they perform. Some studies have included only economic functions, but this is an unnecessary restriction of this approach. Suggestive articles by W. F. Ogburn in 1937 and Chauncy D. Harris in 1943 outlined an approach that did not become widely used until computer technology obviated the trying hand calculations previously necessary. In the last decade an impressive subliterature has thus developed concerning city classification. Many distinct approaches remain, but most start from masses of census-type data on individual cities. In perhaps the most important recent work in this area, Brian Berry standardized 97 variables for 1,762 urban places in the U.S. (2–2). These were then factor-analyzed (by the use of a varimax rotation to extract orthogonal factors). Fourteen factors or "latent dimensions" emerged explaining 77 percent of the variance in the original 97 variables. The first four factors were very similar to others found in analogous studies (3–4)—population size, socioeconomic status, stage in family cycle (mainly young families in suburbs versus older populations in central cities), and nonwhite population—but, as one proceeds down the list, the disadvantages of the approach become more apparent. Perhaps most fundamental is that while the latent dimensions do indeed exhaust most statistical variance, they are not always substantively meaningful. In one sense they inevitably are; that is, insofar as certain dimensions of cities are empirically associated, the analyst should be aware of them. Nevertheless, the separate dimensions emerge in part through the internal logic of the procedure. As virtually nothing in reality is entirely orthogonal, approaches which permit some association to remain (e.g. oblique rotation) are sometimes more useful. One situation, however, where minimal intercorrelation is desirable is in a regression model; causal interpretations of regression normally assume the independent variables to be uncorrelated. Insofar as this assumption is violated, the relative importance of the independent variables, expressed in their regression coefficients, is distorted. From this statistical modeling standpoint, orthogonal factors are thus desirable. But if construction of a model with such orthogonal factors leads to what we have called "model muddling," often the converse difficulty of "precise distortion," arising from somewhat correlated but nevertheless distinct variables, still generates more interpretable results (4–26).

These and other criticisms have been addressed to factor-analytic approaches to city classification (4–26, 2–1). But the approach continues to attract community researchers, perhaps not entirely because of their methodological naïveté. Three situations may be distinguished where the approach can be helpful. In the process of constructing a causal model with several interrelated independent variables, and where their selection is difficult, factor-analytic results remind the researcher of the distinct dimensions in his data which he may want to include. He can then construct closely related models to compare at each stage with alternatives which incorporate the factor analytic dimensions. (This procedure is followed and the results presented and compared in 4–26.)

Second, the researcher moving into a new area— e.g., communities in another region or a different nation-state—may want to compute the basic factor structure to compare with the previous setting. He can then ascertain the distinctiveness of his data set and compare it with others for which such analyses have been performed. Results are now available for cities, regions, and countries throughout the world. Many are reviewed in the Berry volume (2–2); more are in progress (e.g., 4–3).

Third, the researcher may wish to examine the factor structure in selecting individual cities for more intensive analysis. This was done, for example, by Charles Roig and his associates (4–64) before selecting seventeen French towns for further study. We should also note that a number of different, and sometimes sophisticated, data reduction procedures (such as multidimensional scaling) are more appropriate than factor analysis for some purposes, but few have been employed by city researchers to date.[1]

Another approach to isolating community types and dimensions deserves separate mention. It might be labeled the metropolitan specialization tradition, to cover several subspecialties. One is the theoretical perspective on metropolitan differentiation developed by Charles Tiebout and certain other economists

(1–90, 156). Their argument mixes positive and normative elements in that it is meant both as a guide to how things might work and as an approximation of how things do work. One basic concern is to explain how individuals with different preference schedules and different incomes distribute themselves spatially across a metropolitan area. The perspective is clearly that of welfare maximization: each individual (or family unit) should select a residential location which best approximates his optimal amount of police protection, public education, open spaces and parks, access to shopping and museums, etc. These positive elements of a preferences schedule are weighted against the negative elements, such as pollution or high taxes. Each actor may be characterized in these terms concerning his optimal location. Municipalities, following this perspective, should be differentiated throughout metropolitan areas. Then different persons can act on their preference schedules to sort themselves into municipalities containing their preferred amenities and corresponding taxes.

Criticisms of this approach have been many. Generally, it ignores the extremes in preference and income. Certain individuals, especially the poor, will be so limited by their budgetary constraints as to remain far from their optima. Of course this is true in all sorts of decisions—more income implies a lesser budgetary constraint. Insofar as even the poorest person has some choice, however, his preferences affect the alternatives considered. The converse criticism in one sense is that certain individuals with "demanding" preference schedules inevitably remain far from their optima, by virtue of (1) empirical limitations of certain areas, landlocked towns for persons desiring the seaside, for example; and (2) their distinctiveness from other citizens. Traditional market theory holds that any group of citizens can withdraw from existing municipalities to form their "new Jerualem." But the traditional theory ignores transaction costs of getting persons together, as well as economies of scale for many facilities: a town must achieve a sufficient size (and thus include enough persons with similar preference schedules) before many undertakings are viable. The seventy-five residents of Waco, Texas, who long for a nearby opera may be doomed to lifelong frustration.

Among studies on metropolitan phenomena, we find several concerned with the types of municipalities which will cooperate with one another and with specification of the conditions under which this occurs. The policy implications of these questions are clear, and support has been available for many elaborate investigations. Often these have been "postmortem" studies of metropolitan referenda, designed to explain why the referenda failed. Many such referenda (proposing consolidation of municipalities into a single metropolitan government) were held throughout the U.S., largely in the late 1950s. Most failed disastrously. In some instances voters were interviewed concerning reasons for supporting or opposing the referendum; in others, ecological analysis of voting patterns was undertaken. Factor-analytic approaches were used several times to isolate patterns of support or opposition. A consistent result was that affluent suburbs opposed consolidation with other suburbs or central cities to avoid subsidizing public services in these areas. The economic argument was complemented by a desire for different suburbs to retain their distinctive life styles as well as their small size permitting greater citizen involvement and direct access to local leaders. O. P. Williams and his associates (3–127) found suburbs willing to join others for certain specific matters, even if they opposed legal-political consolidation. Technical matters like sewerage were not so hard to agree upon; those more intimately related to life style, like public education, were more often kept autonomous. (See also 3–40, 51, 54, 72.)

We have indicated in this section several approaches to classifying communities. However, since the rationale for doing so is to link certain city dimensions to other variables, such as those in figure 1, we shall return to community characteristics as they impinge on subsequent variables.

A frequent theme in the metropolitan literature is the "suburban exploitation thesis." The argument was put sharply by Amos Hawley in 1951 (4–50). He analyzed expenditure levels of central cities in metropolitan areas across the U.S. In a multivariate model of the sources of variation, he introduced a controversial term: the proportion of residents in the metropolitan area that reside in its suburbs. He found that central cities surrounded by populous suburbs spent more per capita—other variables held constant—than central cities with less populous suburbs. The basic finding was replicated in different areas (4–23), using city employees instead of expenditures (4–57), and in more recent time periods (4–56). But is this relationship adequate evidence to sustain charges of "exploitation"? Ignored in such an assertion are contributions to the central city via a number of indirect or unrecorded sources—for example, receipts of department stores, which in turn pay increased local taxes; transfer payments from state and federal governments increased by suburbanites' taxes; and the increased value of central city land and property, and consequently tax payments, due to proximity of the suburban areas. More studies are needed to trace such matters in detail (see 1–86 for a thorough review of work to date). Ambiguities also remain in defining the value-laden term "exploitation." There seems, however, to be much less disagreement on specific findings than on more general interpretations arising from them.

Over the last two decades the importance of values and cultural characteristics has grown with that of community characteristics. An implicit and consequently vague economic determinism informed many community power studies during the 1950s; values were correspondingly neglected. This has changed for several reasons. We consider some the most important.

The first reason is an extension of the comparative perspective to communities differing dramatically in orientation from each other, initially within the U.S., but increasingly in different national contexts as well. One of the most ambitious projects in this regard is the International Studies of Values in Politics (3–138A, 4–51, 52, 53). Undertaken by researchers in Yugoslavia, India, Poland, and the U.S., the project collected identical data on value configurations of some thirty local leaders (elected, appointed, administrative) in thirty communities in each country. These were summarized in nine basic value scales, such as concern for economic development, conflict avoidance, participation, national (versus local) commitment, honesty, and economic equality. Some rather dramatic and often unexpected differences appeared: the American leaders were less concerned with avoiding conflict than the Yugoslavs or especially the Indians; American and Yugoslav leaders were more concerned with encouraging citizen participation than the Poles or Indians; but the Indians and Yugoslavs were committed to more fundamental changes than the Americans, especially in matters of economic equality. How is one to interpret such variations? Controls can be introduced, for example, for basic individual and national differences in income and education. But much variance, it seems, remains. Many observers conclude that at least some of the variation resides in differing value-orientations. These in turn may be traced back historically to demographic, economic, or other factors, but at one point in time, given such salient cross-national differences, the value dimension seems hard to ignore.

We have already discussed studies of metropolitan differentiation which have sharpened the focus on value differences across communities.

The introduction of values as distinct, central, independent variables also helps resolve several theoretical problems which remained implicit in many earlier studies. Perhaps most important is the analytical linkage which values provide across the different variables in figure 1. That is, as one considers differences in community characteristics, leadership, and policy outputs, what specific dimensions of these variables should be related to each other? The need for such common dimensions is especially apparent in considering policy outputs. To go beyond higher or lower levels of outputs in terms of dollars or units of housing constructed, for example, it is important to link the output with distinct value patterns of different community subgroups.

Theoretically suggestive answers to certain value-related questions are found in work emerging from traditions like "the economic theory of democracy." The term became diffused as the title for the popular volume by Anthony Downs, but it was a direct extension of ideas developed for analysis of the private sector. The model included the rational voter qua consumer, and the rational aspirant to political office qua producer of campaign promises, ideology, and specific policies. If one grants the most fundamental assumption of the work, that policy differences may be arrayed along a single dimension, then voters and candidates place themselves on different points along the continuum. Each voter should support the candidate closest to his preferred point. Then if the number of voters at each point is arrayed to create a frequency distribution, support for each candidate can be estimated by the voters' distance from his policy position. It is clear that the most desirable point for obtaining votes—normally the winning position—is the median point of the continuum; it minimizes the distance between the candidate and voters. Space does not permit consideration of the many suggestive refinements emerging from this line of thinking; some of the most interesting may be found in the new journal *Public Choice*, many articles in the *American Political Science Review* over the last decade, and scattered in other books and journals. *Public Choice* also has included several bibliographies which can guide the interested reader to further materials. We list only some of the most important names: Duncan Black, Kenneth Arrow, James M. Buchanan, Gordon Tullock, Otto Davis, Peter Ordeshook, William Riker, Martin Shubik, Mancur Olson, James S. Coleman.

Analysis of values can also help answer certain recurrent problems in community decision making. One concerns the interrelated issues of "nondecisions" and "who benefits," raised by such writers as Bachrach, Baratz, Scoble, and Lipsky (1–6, 5–14). In the absence of specific decisions in a community or issue area, can one suggest that nondecisions are any more unexpected than the absence of a volcano in every main street? How can one identify such nondecisions, or, proceeding further, how can one suggest that various sectors of the community "benefit" or "lose" from certain nondecisions, or even from explicit decisions, for that matter? Values of different community sectors may be examined to provide part of the answer to these questions. First, values of leading decision makers can be compared with those of community citizens, especially those interested in or affected by decisions in the specific issue area. If differences emerge, the researcher can isolate the areas where leaders apparently acted on different value premises from those of the sectors affected. If leaders respond differentially to different sectors of the population, one can suggest that the sectors whose values are most adequately represented in community decisions benefit more than other sectors. And if virtually no decisions are being taken in an area, but a clear dissensus exists between the values of an important sector of citizens and community leaders, one can suggest that the nondecision is at odds with the values of that sector.

Still, the researcher is doubtless on firmer ground, and doing more than recording random noises, if he can demonstrate instances where a representative of the value in question attempted to convert the non-decision into a decision, and the result was an explicit negative decision, i.e., a decision not to implement the suggested action. With the increasing range of political positions offered by different would-be leaders during the 1960s, particularly in the U.S., it has been much easier empirically to study negative decisions rather than nondecisions. In recent years, when these negative decisions have been the clear result of the community majority against an unhappy minority, critics have been more hesitant to invoke nondecisions or the mobilization of bias; the more consistent social critics have attacked the basics of majority rule.

One can still raise the issue discussed under such headings as "false consciousness" or mistaken interests. That is, do certain individuals act as they do, not because it is "best" for them (ignoring momentarily how to define best), but because they have been misled by the mass media or the bourgeoisie or the technostructure? In its most general form, this question is hardly susceptible to systematic analysis, but certain recent developments have given us a theoretical handle with which to grasp at least part of the problem. We refer here to the extensions of exchange theory to deal with institutional structures and value patterns (1–78). Consider two actors who exchange equal amounts of resources, defined as things considered important by actors in the same social system —money, information, control of manpower, etc. As scarce commodities desired by members of a social system, resources may be calibrated and analyzed in the same way that money is in an economic system. If a person begins to receive more than he gives in

turn, we can expect that he will have to make good
this imbalance in some way, if not immediately or
materially, then at some future point or in the realm
of values. This basic idea can be adapted to different
community actors, each of whom can be assigned a
payoff coefficient,

$$PC_i = O_i/I_i$$

where O_i and I_i are defined respectively as the outputs
which actor i receives from the polity, and the inputs
which he contributes to it, both measured in resources.
Each social system will tend over time to institution-
alize a PC. Then, when any single actor receives or
contributes more than expected in terms of the PC,
his imbalance may be made good by his accepting
the values of those others in the polity who make a
disproportionate contribution of resources, or him
having the chance to diffuse his own values when
his own contribution exceeds expectations. Over long
time periods, therefore, if such imbalances in exchange persist, we may expect the values of "generous" actors (United Fund contributors, perhaps) to
be accepted by others in the community. See 1–78
for further discussion.

Before leaving values we may mention problems
of operationalization and measurement. Attitude surveys using standardized questionnaires are probably
the most widely preferred, and in the last decade an
increasing number of community studies have collected value data for local leaders as well as citizens.
Comparisons between leaders and citizens are thus
possible, and have been made in several instances
(3–144, 159). Content analyses of speeches and other
documents have also been completed in conjunction

with the International Studies of Values in Politics (3–138A) and by Jambrek (4–54) in studying Yugoslav city council decisions.

Fundamental problems remain in the area of values —we need mention only public and private regardingness, immediate gratification, and citizen satisfaction with policy outputs as areas where work is in progress. A substantial amount of work has been completed in these areas in the last decade; still more seems likely in the next.

3   Centralization of Power and Decision Making— and Decentralization

After Floyd Hunter used *Community Power Structure* (3–76) as the title of his doctoral dissertation in 1953, the term "power structure" became widely used by scholars as well as, eventually, the general public. Unfortunately, however, referents varied from the Nazi party to progressive American parents, and from the existence of a slight imbalance of resources to consistent social actions. Warm debates developed in the early 1960s concerning such concepts as "power structure," "power elite," and "pluralism," which often remained confused. Contradictory empirical results and conceptual discussions which speak past each other are clarified if a firm distinction is maintained between power and influence.

Power is conceived as the potential ability of an actor or actors to select, to change, and to attain the goals of a social system. The key term here is potential; actors with access to resources may or may not choose to activate these resources. *Influence*, by contrast, is the exercise of power that brings about change in a social system. *Resources* such as money, knowledge, technical skills, control of manpower, and the right to vote constitute the bases of power; but it is their application in specific decisions that comprises the exercise of influence. From these distinctions it

27

follows that a *power structure* is a patterned distribution of power in social system, while a *decision-making structure* is a patterned distribution of influence.

Hunter was unfortunately vague on many conceptual issues, but he made a major contribution in what has come to be called the reputational approach or method. It basically consisted of asking a panel of judges to rank-order individuals "who in your opinion are the most influential persons . . . influential from the point of view of *ability* to lead others" (3–76, page 258, italics added). Those persons mentioned were interviewed in turn; they were presented the list of persons compiled and asked to rank-order those on the list and to add to it where appropriate. Rankings in terms of degree of intimacy or frequency of communication could then be established using the sociometric techniques developed in the early 1950s. Persons consistently chosen—in Hunter's Atlanta, generally businessmen and professionals—were considered members of the power structure.

The simplicity and apparent precision of Hunter's approach led to its frequent imitation during the 1950s. It nevertheless contained two basic weaknesses. First, Hunter confused power and influence: the method isolated powerful but not necessarily influential individuals. And in loose discussion of his findings Hunter and others using the reputational approach often assumed that the powerful could and did have their way in most matters. Nevertheless, how, when, and to what degree power was in fact converted into influence was virtually ignored. Although one could find long and impressive series of sociometric networks, there was virtually never an accompanying discussion of actual decisions or processes by which decisions were reached. Second, Hunter and most following in his footsteps failed to specify the scope of power for different leaders. If not stated explicitly, it was often implied that leaders were powerful across all or at least most important community issues. The reputational approach, however, in unrefined form, did not specify the degree to which different leaders were powerful in different issue areas.

Two important studies appeared in 1961 which avoided these weaknesses: Robert Dahl's *Who Governs?* and Edward Banfield's *Political Influence* (3–59, 47). Although Dahl and Banfield discussed resources available to community actors, and in this sense portrayed the power structures of New Haven and Chicago, their major concern was influence—how specific decisions were made in different issue areas. Less explicit in their methods than Hunter, they combined materials from newspapers, documents, interviews, and participant observation. Their analysis of these diverse materials in order to reconstruct specific decisions, however, permits their methodology to be characterized as decisional. Analysis of such concrete decisions leads naturally to comparisons of the degree to which leaders active in one issue area are also active in others. Comparing influence patterns in mayoral elections, urban renewal, hospital construction, and similar issue areas, Dahl and Banfield generally concluded that few actors overlapped across issue areas. In both New Haven and Chicago, the major exception was the mayor and his staff, who were central to most issue areas studied.

By the early 1960s some 166 case studies of individual communities had been completed in the U.S.; but many were considered unreliable by researchers of differing conceptual or methodological persuasions. Indeed, the quantity of research completed, and the continuing disagreements among certain researchers, led some observers to feel that the subject was especially appropriate for the sociology of knowledge. We will deal with these issues in chapter 6. Here we point out simply that many disagreements were overblown, in part because of the absence of an accepted distinction between power and influence, each demanding separate procedures for operationalization. Disagreements were also encouraged, however, by the narrowness of the case study. If each researcher investigated in detail only a single community, he had difficulty conceiving of or demonstrating how things might vary elsewhere. Pride, naturally, led each to maintain that his town was more representative than, and his approach superior to, those of others. Certain younger scholars entering the field at this time, however, felt that many disagreements could be resolved through more systematic comparisons of communities. Empirical studies of two, three, or four communities were published in these years (3–42, 106), but to test propositions about the relative effects of different community characteristics, it is necessary to have a data base of several dozen cases. This reasoning led initially to coding the case studies and comparing the results quantitatively. This was done by several researchers, using generally similar approaches but different samples (5–15, 18, 19, 24, 26; 1–107).

The relatively generous funding for social science research in the U.S. in the late 1960s also made possible large-scale empirical efforts. A leading example is the Permanent Community Sample: a national sample of communities where data are recorded continually, permitting cross-sectional and time series analysis (2–16, 4–25). The initial study included fifty-one communities, in each of which eleven informants were interviewed by representatives of the National Opinion Research Center at the University of Chicago.

Both the quantitative comparisons of case studies and initial work on the fifty-one communities were devoted to isolating community correlates of centralization. That is, if one conceives of power and decision-making structures varying along a continuum from centralized to decentralized, different communities may be compared on this continuum. The continuum was operationalized in the quantitative comparisons of case studies in classifications ranging, for example, from "pyramidal," to "coalitional," to "amorphous." However, ambiguities of many case studies made difficult separation of power and decision-making structures, as well as, unfortunately often, specification of the precise degree of centralization. Because of questions raised about the impact of the researchers discipline or use of the reputational or decisional approach, controls for discipline and method were used in several comparisons. Nevertheless, relations between community characteristics and centralization were weak; although some were significant using bivariate statistics, they seldom remained significant in multivariate models. In the one study that used a regression model, sixteen independent variables explained only 10 percent of the variance in centralization (5–15). In the fifty-one-communities study, however, directly comparable questions were posed in each community. These concerned urban renewal, mayoral elections, air pollution control, and antipoverty activities, and were presented using both issue-specific reputational and ersatz decisional formats (4–7, 25). Identical questions were posed to informants in identical positions in each community. An Index of Decentralization was then created based on the number of different actors involved in different issue areas. The success in obtaining comparable data and in reducing "noise" in the findings was suggested by more powerful results than those for the quantitative comparisons of case studies: 46 percent of the variance in the decentralization index was explained by an eight-variable regression model.

Where relationships are isolated by the use of different methods and samples, and results begin to cumulate, it is especially interesting to compare findings from different studies. Table 1 displays the basic results from both quantitative comparisons of case studies and the fifty-one-communities study. The following general formulation subsumes many of these findings: *The greater the horizontal differentiation in a social system, the greater the differentiation between potential elites, and the more decentralized the power and decision-making structures.* One demographic characteristic generally associated with structural differentiation is population size: *the larger the number of inhabitants in a community, the greater the structural differentiation* is a basic idea linked to the general formulation above (4–4). Ignoring momentarily the intervening linkages, we see in Table 1 the association between population size and decentralization. Gilbert found a positive relation; Walton and Aiken found no consistent pattern; in the fifty-one-

Table 1. Relations between Community Characteristics and Decentralization

	Gilbert[a]	Walton[b]	Aiken[c]	Clark[d]
Population size	+	0	0	+
Economic diversification	0	0	0	+
Absentee ownership		+	+	
Industrialization	0	0	0	0
Military installations				−
Index of Reform Government				−
Nonpartisan elections	−			
City manager	0	0	−	
Direct election of mayor			+	
Competing political parties		+		+
Civic voluntary activity				±
Educational level of citizens	0		0	±

+ = positive relationship
− = negative relationship
0 = no significant relationship
± = mixed findings depending on model specification
blank = relationship not reported

a. Gilbert (1968), 5–18. Data are for 166 communities, coded from earlier case studies. Findings are zero-order dichotomous relationships based on Fisher's exact test of probability, .10 or higher in significance with discipline and methodology of the researcher controlled.

b. Walton (1970), 5–26. Data are for 61 communities from 39 studies. Findings are zero-order relationships, with significance based on Fisher's exact test, computed from Q statistics and gammas. Control introduced for method of data collection.

c. Aiken (1970), 1–107. Data are for 31 communities from previous case studies, supplemented from other sources. Findings are significant at at least the .10 level using partial correlation coefficients with methodology and discipline of the researcher controlled.

d. Clark (1968b, 1973), 1–57, 4–7, 25, 26. Data are for 51 communities, collected by NORC interviewers and from other sources. Findings are zero-order correlation coefficients and regression coefficients, significant at at least the .10 level.

Source: Terry N. Clark, "The structure of community influence." In Harlan H. Hahn, ed., *People and Politics in Urban Society* (Beverly Hills, Cal.: Sage Publications, 1972), p. 291. (Modifications added.)

communities study a clear positive zero-order relation emerged.

The broad concept of structural differentiation in the formulation can be specified in several distinct institutional arrangements.

Structural differentiation in the economic sphere is tapped in good part by economic diversification. In the fifty-one-communities study, when centralization was regressed on economic diversification and population size, diversification alone remained significant, just as we would expect theoretically. Next, to refer back to our discussion of vertical linkages, recall the deduction of Walton's work: when vertical linkages are reinforced in a situation where previously weak, greater decentralization is likely. This idea is supported in the positive relation between absentee ownership of economic enterprises and decentralization. Industrialization, measured by the presence of industry, showed no relation to decentralization. More important for decentralization, however, are indirect effects of industrialization: wealth, education, and especially increased time for leisure and civic activities. The military installation variable emerged from the factor-analytic approach of Berry discussed above;

it remained negatively associated with decentralization even in a multivariate model including eight other
variables.

Turning from economic to legal-political variables,
our formulation suggests the import of factors linked
to differentiation. In American cities, legal variations
concern primarily the so-called reform characteristics.
Conceived as a unified program, nonpartisan elections, at-large electoral constituencies, and the professional city manager were adopted by many cities
after the early twentieth century. To "reform" city
government, these changes aimed to weaken the small
ward and machine-oriented mayor and city council,
and to place considerable authority in the hands of
the city manager. In the fifty-one-communities study,
an Index of Reform Government was computed including these three characteristics. It showed the expected negative relation to decentralization, as did
the individual reform characteristics analyzed in the
other studies.

Competing political parties are another manifesta-
tion of structural differentiation; Walton and Clark
found them positively related to decentralization. Active voluntary organizations should show the same
relation, but the results were inconclusive here. This
relation is confounded by that with education. Cities
with more educated persons are more likely to have
reformed institutions; and these in turn are strongly
associated with centralization. Hence the difficulties
of disentangling the empirical relations.

In general, then, these findings from different
studies and samples tend to support the generaliza-
tion that structural differentiation promotes decentralization.

A few remarks are in order on a second usage of
the term "decentralization," and the corresponding
issues which it raises. When decentralization was introduced in 4–4, it was chosen as a neutral, non-
ideological term to avoid such banners as pluralism
or monolithic or power elite, and to make explicit
the idea of a continuum. Just a few years later, however, decentralization became the slogan for many
proponents of greater neighborhood authority, especially for poor neighborhoods in large cities. Many
ideological issues were raised in this debate—which,
of course, was by no means restricted to cities or to
the United States. Formal organizations, especially
universities and industries, and national governments
in many parts of the world, were attacked in the late
1960s because of inadequate "participation" or "decentralization." In the U.S. these concerns were
heightened in several federal programs of the Johnson years, especially the Community Action Projects
and Model Cities programs, with their legal and ideological emphasis on participation and decentralization. Much of this debate took place, as one would
expect, without any awareness of earlier work bearing
on the issues discussed. A few efforts were made,
however, to elaborate the parallels between the two
meanings of decentralization (1–94, 124).

One parallel concerns the community correlates of
decentralization, as just reviewed. Findings at the
municipality level would seem at least a good place
to begin in considering analogous phenomena at the
neighborhood level; the same applies to linkages between centralization and outputs. As regards the
substantive meaning of centralization and leadership,
the long discussions of democratic theory—at least

from Schumpeter to *Who Governs?*—should be re-
membered: democracy very seldom has been or can
be coterminous with direct participation in formal
decisions. This point in turn raises the issue of the
optimal size of decision-making units, the subject of
Robert Dahl's presidential address to the American
Political Science Association (1–94). Dahl pointed
out the inevitable tradeoff between the importance
of decisions which can be taken by a given decision-
making unit (family, neighborhood, municipality,
metropolitan, national or world government) and the
degree of involvement or impact which any individual
can expect. If we were all Robinson Crusoes we could
be reasonably autonomous, but we could not expect
to change the course of activities outside our little
islands. On the other hand, direct discussion and
significant involvement by thousands and millions in
every decision of large social systems is simply in-
feasible. Hence the absurdity of an unqualified popu-
list conception of democracy in large complicated
societies. On the other hand, this conclusion should
not trouble the less than highly politicized person,
i.e. most persons. Study after study has shown that
very, very few persons care enough about politics at
any level to do more than vote irregularly (e.g.
1–105). Many speaking and writing on the subject
have still demanded smaller units to permit greater
participation. Most discussions—even Dahl's—of the
desirability of greater participation, neighborhood decentralization, and optimal city size, have unfortunately proceeded by considering the relations only
between the participation level and the size of the
unit, while ignoring most others. But the world, alas,
and most of its citizens have many concerns in addi-

tion to citizen participation. This observation suggests the desirability of considering alternative, and enlarged, frameworks for evaluating decentralization.

One effort was made several years ago by O. D. Duncan. He drew together numerous statements by architects, planners, and others offering prescriptions concerning the optimal size for a city, or at least concerning facilities which optimally should be present. He then estimated the number of residents who would have to be brought together to support these various facilities. The results indicated the optimal size for a city under a variety of different assumptions.

An alternative approach was suggested in 1–124 to serve at any rate as a useful normative model. Consider the set of citizens in a given area. Obtain from them their preferences concerning all things which they seek to do alone or which depend on social relations. Results could be listed for each individual in the form of what economists term a utility function. Its elements could be assigned scores to indicate the relative importance accorded them by the individual. Each element could then be linked to the optimal size of the social unit in which it could be obtained. If the same population were used, estimates could be derived from the empirical frequency with which such things as a movie theater or zoo are found in communities of different size; levels at which economies of scale begin and end could be correspondingly calculated. One element in each individual's utility function would be participation in decision making, but (as a means) it should be kept separate from (the end of) obtaining certain services which may result from such participation. Alternative means, such as surveys, may then be considered. The relative importance of participation could be weighted and combined with the other elements in the utility functions of different individuals to obtain their optimal city size. The obvious point in this scheme is that economies of scale for one service, e.g., opera, should be sacrificed for another, e.g., participation, only if the individual values participation over the opera. Assigning weights to the opera, participation, and other elements, would permit computation of a weighted optimum. Clearly, the methodological obstacles to realization of this program are huge; but it should be considered as a possibly more realistic, if more complicated, normative solution to the problem of how to decentralize (or centralize).

The major experiments with decentralization over the last decade provide a marvelous laboratory for developing our understanding of types and amounts of participation. The apparent disappointment, if not bitterness, which many Johnson programs left with their participants, not to mention the average citizen or members of the Nixon administration, may encourage writing off the whole exercise as an enormous failure. This would be truly unfortunate. What is needed is neither uncritical support nor critical rejection, but qualified assessment of the strengths and weaknesses of different programs. It remains to be seen if any of the many evaluations to date can confront the basic issues with enough rigor to persuade skeptics. In any case these evaluations, and the participants' experiences, provide valuable raw materials for dealing with the broader issues of decentralization and participation; their balanced interpretation remains a major task for the next decade.

4   Leadership Characteristics: Resources and Their Consequences

Leadership in our framework (see figure 1) refers to characteristics of the most central actors in the community power or decision-making structure. Basic dimensions are occupational characteristics (e.g., businessmen, civic leaders, political party leaders), social backgrounds (e.g., father's occupation, educational level), and values (e.g., conservative-liberal). What theory and empirical findings relate variations along these dimensions to other variables in our framework?

One idea developed considerably over the last decade is that of resources. Writers from Aristotle through Marx and Weber dealt with constitutions or the means of production or bureaucratic structures facilitating influence by different types of actors. But it was Harold Lasswell (1–36) and especially Robert Dahl who considered these varied structures and properties under a common heading. Dahl made many contributions, including the concept of "slack," stressing that there is often room for greater activation of resources in a social system. He spoke too of "pyramiding" resources—a process by which an actor could activate his resources for influence in a given issue area. Starting from an explicit list of resources, he analyzed the ways and manner in which various re-

41

sources were differentially stratified and how they could be directly or indirectly employed to exercise influence (1–15, 16, 3–59).

Talcott Parsons was one of the most influential writers on power and influence in the mid-1960s, and he went still further than Dahl in analyzing power in abstract terms. His emphasis on the generality of resources, and the ways in which they could interpenetrate and link together different social systems, was important. Analyzing resources as a circulating medium analogous to money, he was led to assert the inappropriateness of a zero-sum conception of power —where one actor's loss is precisely balanced by gains on the part of others (1–44, 45, 46).

It was by building on such writers as Dahl and Parsons that several subsequent refinements were introduced in considering resources. The simple labeling of resources as a distinctive analytical category was important. This apparently elementary step encouraged many subsequent developments. When resources are conceived as a distinct category, their contrast with influence, and corresponding (mere) potentiality, is emphasized. Explaining why different actors make use of their various resources then becomes an explicit problem. One can formulate the matter in terms of the following simple equation:

$$I = p_a R$$

where I is influence, p_a is an activation probability, and R is resources. That is, influence is a function of resources only insofar as the probability of resource activation is above zero. But even then actors with substantial resources may not have their way. Consider an elementary example. Assume only two actors

attempt to influence a mayoral election: a steel factory
and a local Democratic party. The steel factory has
far more resources, ten times to be exact. But the
Democratic party is organized for political struggles
and is very concerned about the election. The steel
factory is ready to contribute a total of $200,000 in
cash, personnel, time, etc. But this represents only
2 percent of the steel factory's resources. The Democratic party, on the other hand, will invest half its
resources in the election. The situation for each actor
is then as follows:

Steel Factory	*Democratic Party*
$R = \$10,000,000$	$R = \$1,000,000$
$p_a = .02$	$p_a = .50$
$I = .02 \times \$10,000,000$	$I = .50 \times \$1,000,000$
$I = \$200,000$	$I = \$500,000$

If influence is measured by use of a *numéraire* with
a dollar sign, then in our example the Democratic
party would win.

Let us consider ways to make this example more
sophisticated. We used a single equation for each
actor in just one issue area. Equations could be written with subscripts for each actor and issue area.
Further, R is by no means homogeneous. Our example implicitly aggregated all the actor's resources
to create R; but often it is the particular distribution
of resources, $r_1, r_2 \ldots r_n$, that is crucial in distinguishing actors. (This is true as there are inevitable transaction costs in converting one resource into another.)
One may then proceed analytically—or empirical
actors may act—using two different strategies. The
first is to consider the configuration of resources essential for a given end. Assume, for example, that

one wishes to build new housing in a slum area. Urban renewal legislation and funding are available, as are developers and capital. One strategy for building the housing is to form a coalition with enough actors for all necessary resources to be found in the coalition. This approach leads to considering attributes of actors joining a coalition, and principles by which coalitions may be created, maintained, and extended. Arthur Stinchcombe has followed this approach in a reinterpretation of Banfield's *Political Influence*. He lists the resources of the major actors (see table 2) before turning to the requirements of the major projects and considering possible coalitions. The literature on these issues is just in the process of being linked to that of community power and decision making. The game-theoretic background of coalition work links it with collective decision-making studies discussed above. *Public Choice, Behavioral Science,* and certain social psychological journals have carried material along these lines. Martin Shubik, James S. Coleman, and Gerald H. Kramer are doing important work relating the abstract formulations to more institutional phenomena.

A second strategy for this problem considers not each distinct actor and his distribution of resources, but the resources alone. That is, housing may normally be built using developers, but this is not mandatory. Instead of considering how to bring a developer into a coalition, one can ask what particular resources he brings, and how they are accessible through other channels. On a higher analytical level, consider a matrix of resources as shown in table 3. Each resource may be converted into any other: but at what price? How easily can dollars be exchanged for con-

Table 2. The (Disposable) Power Resources of Elites

Elites	Eminent domain	Suitable sites	Bond issue (millions of dollars)	Publicity (circulation in thousands)	Money (millions of dollars)	Taxing power	Licenses	Tariff privileges, etc.
Downtown business		X		50	400		X	
Uptown business				50	100		X	
City machine	X	X	200	200	10		X	
State government	X		50	200	20	X	X	
Good-government crowd			50	100				
Federal government	X			100	500	X		X
Chicago Tribune			200	1,000	1			

Source: Arthur L. Stinchcombe, Constructing Social Theories (New York: Harcourt, Brace, and World, 1968) p. 192.

Table 3. Convertibility Matrix of Resources

	Money and credit	Control over jobs	Control of mass media	High social status	Knowledge and technical skills	Popularity and personal qualities
Money and credit	—	H	H	H	H	H
Control over jobs	H	—	L	M	L	M
Control of mass media	M	L	—	M	M	H
High social status	H	L	L	—	L	M
Knowledge and technical skills	H	M	M	M	—	M
Popularity and personal qualities	M	L	L	H	L	—
Legality	L	L	L	M	L	M
Subsystem solidarity	M	L	L	M	L	H
The right to vote	L	L	L	L	L	L
Social access to community leaders	M	M	M	M	M	M
Commitments of followers	M	L	L	M	L	H
Manpower and control of organizations	H	L	L	M	L	M
Control over interpretation of values	L	M	L	H	L	H
"Selling price"	25	17	16	26	16	28

Legend:	Symbol	Mean
	H	high
	M	mediu
	L	low

Source: Terry N. Clark, ed., *Community Structure and Decision-Making: Con* *tive Analyses* (Scranton, Pa.: Intext-Chandler Publishing Company, 1968), p.

The right to vote	Social access to community leaders	Commitments of followers	Manpower and control of organizations	Control over interpretation of values	"Buying power"
M	H	H	H	M	32
L	L	H	H	L	21
M	M	H	L	H	23
M	H	M	L	M	22
M	M	M	L	M	25
M	H	H	M	M	25
H	M	M	L	M	19
M	M	H	M	M	23
—	L	L	L	M	15
H	—	M	M	M	25
M	M	—	M	L	22
M	M	M	—	L	21
H	M	M	L	—	24
26	25	28	20	21	

Score
3
2
1

trol of the mass media? More easily, it seems, than
converting high social status into knowledge and technical skills. Such specific comparisons are obviously
only approximations, but they remain useful in illustrating the underlying phenomenon: wholesale exchanges of resources. Such wholesale exchanges of
resources can permit an actor or group of actors to
acquire the resources essential to achieve their ends.
Wholesale exchanges may be contrasted with retail
exchanges, i.e. conversions of resources into something which, at one time period at least, is an end
for the actor. Leading examples are increasing social
prestige, institutionalizing values, and exercising influence. Scores may be assigned different resources to
represent their prices in each of these retail "markets"
as for the wholesale market. Composite indices or
prices may then be computed for each resource; results along these lines are presented in 4–4, chapter 3.

Working from a similar perspective, James S.
Coleman (1–58) has analyzed a situation widely
debated during the 1960s: that of a social sector
disadvantaged in most resources. His major example
was blacks in the U.S., but the framework is readily
adapted to other situations. Besides the wholesale
and retail exchanges just discussed, Coleman focused
on "arenas of action." To analyze pressure points of
a social system, he cross-classified a list of resources
with these arenas of action (see table 4). He then
reviewed some eleven theories or policies for social
change under debate at the time, including the input
resources essential for each policy, the arenas of
action (where input resources are converted into
something else) strategic for the theory, and the output resources enhanced by the conversion. A scheme

Table 4. Input Resources to Arenas of Action

Input resource	Arenas of action									
	Occupation	Family socialization	Family consumption	School	Local community	Elections	Legislature	Courts	Civil rights groups	Black power groups
Personal resources	X	X	X	X	X	X			X	X
Family cohesion		X	X	X					X	
Community cohesion		X			X					
Political movement organization								X	X	X
Jobs	X									
Money			X							
Goods			X							
Services	X	X		X						
Freedom of action	X			X	X	X			X	X
Demographic concentration					X	X				
Legal rules, laws					X			X	X	X
Political representation							X			

Source: James S. Coleman, *Resources for Social Change* (New York: Wiley-Interscience, 1971), p. 85.

such as that of Table 4 permits a group considering alternative policies to evaluate its available resources, choose among policies and arenas of action, and assess some probably consequences.[2]

Coleman's "voluntaristic" portrayal of resource activation is a refreshing antidote to many exaggeratedly deterministic writings on power. But one can still usefully consider structural factors likely to encourage greater activation of resources. That is, Dahl's concept of slack and Parsons' emphasis on the inappropriateness of a zero-sum game remind us of freedom of action; but when and why should different actors begin to pyramid their resources, converting their power into influence? We have little theory in this area; but we have a few general hypotheses. Briefly, one idea is that *"the more dependent a community sector is on other sectors of the community for crucial inputs and outputs, the more that sector is likely to become involved (and activate its resources) in community decision-making"* (1–57). The idea is illustrated perhaps most simply by considering two communities, one with an economy dominated by absentee-owned corporations which buy raw materials, set labor contracts, and sell in national markets, and a second with locally owned enterprises which depend on local raw materials and local labor contracts, and sell to local buyers. The hypothesis suggests that enterprises in the second community would be more involved in local political and social affairs. Other community actors may be compared along these same dimensions. Mayors and local political actors are crucially dependent on the local community for inputs (votes) and outputs (delivery of services, etc.); so is a newspaper, printing largely local news (and advertising) and selling it locally. Mayors and newspapers, consistent with our hypothesis, are also among the most active of all actors in community affairs; but obviously they are often far from possessing the most resources; hence their high activation probabilities. A second idea is that *"the greater the differentiation within a particular community sector, the more decentralized the sectoral decision-making structure, and the lower the sectoral involvement in community decision-making"* (1–57). To consider again the economic sector, an economically diversified community is less likely to have economic actors important in politics than is a company town; in a company town one need not expend effort to overcome internal conflicts of interest and just to communicate information essential for concerted action as in an economically diversified community. Analogous reasoning seems to apply to other community sectors. Some twenty more specific propositions, mainly concerning newspapers, have been elaborated in conjunction with these two general hypotheses in 1–57.

A few comments on measuring resources and related issues. Some resources in principle are reasonably easily measured—e.g., income, education, capital, control of manpower. But although such data are often collected by national census bureaus for certain units (state, county, municipality, sometimes by ethnicity), such disaggregation is seldom sufficient, for it is seldom coterminous with distinct political actors. Hence the necessity, generally, for the researcher to collect such data in an original survey. Here it is useful to introduce a distinction between what we may term "base resources"—money, education, social

status, etc., as just analyzed—and "reputational resources"—the latter measured by variations of the
reputational approach. That is, since the reputational
format inquires about the potential or probable influence of specific actors, not about their access to "base
resources," the two must be distinguished. Three
transformation matrices can then be constructed: one
showing conversion of base resources into reputational
resources, a second of base resources into influence,
and a third of reputational resources into influence.
Such transformational matrices could be constructed
separately by actor, issue area, and resource, where
appropriate; scores could be compared by actor type
(e.g., mayor) across communities and related to
community characteristics as well. Such matrices
would provide empirical estimates for the entries
shown in the tables of Stinchcombe, Clark, and Coleman above. Preliminary results along these lines are
presented in 1–57. The articulation of different sets
of variables along common dimensions has already
been stressed. Leadership should correspondingly be
operationalized on dimensions with as many possible
linkages to other variables in the analytical framework. To date, the most ambitious empirical studies
have compared citizens' values with leaders' values
on dimensions like conservatism-liberalism; very few
have taken the next step of linking these variables to
policy outputs.

5   Policy Outputs

It was dissatisfaction with the traditional concern of "Who governs?" that led to an emphasis on "With what effects?" This shift away from the *process* of decision making and governance toward the *policy consequences* was by no means unique to community studies but characterized work in many substantive areas, especially among political scientists. Specifically at the community level, concern with "delivery of services" and satisfaction of citizen demands became accentuated in the 1960s. Simultaneously comparative community studies were growing in importance; and as outputs clearly varied across communities, they seemed important to explain with other community characteristics. Finally, the vastly increased federal programs varied dramatically across cities; researchers asked why. Federal officials and other observers also wondered what effects different forms of transfers had on local activities. When did a federal grant substitute for local spending, when was it a clear net addition, and when did it encourage greater local activity? These interrelated questions generated substantial interest in policy outputs over the last decade.

As in other areas, concern with a new variable led researchers first to examine previous work in the

area. The major example in this case was work by
public finance economists, often published in the *National Tax Journal*. After Solomon Fabricant (4–37)
studied state and local expenditures in 1952, many
others followed in his footsteps. His and many subsequent studies took the combined expenditures for
state and local governments by state and regressed
them on selected state characteristics. In Fabricant's
model the three main explanatory variables were
population density, income, and urbanization. Several state level studies by political scientists built on
this tradition in the 1960s, but they also often considered V. O. Key's hypothesis that competitive party
structures should increase spending. When expenditures were regressed on various measures of party
competitiveness, along with wealth variables, however, competitiveness was seldom as important as the
wealth measures. This encouraged much debate about
the import of the political process as a contribution
to policy making. The results were often interpreted
following the perspective of "incrementalism" inspired by the theoretical work of Charles E. Lindblom and by the national budgeting studies of Aaron
Wildavsky. Several persons at Carnegie–Mellon University linked the incrementalist perspective with
simulation models of budgetary decisions; the major
example at the city level was that of Patrick Crecine
(3–58). Another urban simulation model was developed by Jay Forrester at M.I.T. While Crecine estimated his equations using budgetary data for three
cities over a twenty-year period, Forrester used virtually no empirical data; he still extrapolated his
model to cover hundreds of years. The two are interesting to contrast. Crecine's results, starkly put, were

that budgetary decisions consisted largely of adding a percentage increase to previous expenditures. Population expansion and turnover, changes of government, and political pressures of all sorts were less central to Crecine than the relations of the mayor or city manager with the city council and the heads of each agency, who negotiated relative budgetary increases. This highly internal, bureaucratic, and essentially nonpolitical model was dissatisfying to many who felt that political forces played a more central role.

Forrester's results had something of a deterministic resonance as well, but in almost the opposite sense. Instead of incremental change, his extended time perspective telescoped centuries into a few minutes of computer simulation. Briefly, urbanization, industrialization, and population growth were eventually accompanied by an increase in "underemployed" persons; they drew on the local government for welfare, housing, etc., forcing up taxes and driving out the more affluent. This cycle was likely to be disastrous if permitted to continue, Forrester argued, unless stringent measures to reverse it were adopted; massive urban renewal programs, replacing low income housing with new industries, were his basic recommendation.

Although these simulation studies were dramatically different in substance, both were commendable in their explicitness. Both were based on specific equations linking the variables in the models, which permitted simulating results over time, and projections under a variety of assumptions. As first efforts, however, their explicitness and simplifications (mainly by deleting whole sets of variables) led both studies to be sharply attacked. We do not review details of the studies or their criticisms; space forbids. These details are less important at this point than the general perspective encouraged by such models; they seem destined to frequent imitation in the years ahead. The approach is more common in economics than other disciplines, but as urban economists are increasingly concerned to build political and social variables into their models, possibilities for interdisciplinary teamwork are encouraging. Several projects are in progress along these lines involving Jerome Rothenberg at M.I.T., John Kain at Harvard, Irma Adelman at Northwestern, and Harvey Perloff at U.C.L.A.

The incrementalist approach differs from a perspective that might be labeled sociopolitical in that it seeks to explain variation in policy outputs using social and political variables (such as shown in figure 1), instead of invoking primarily administrative repetitiveness. Incrementalists have often studied an agency or agencies over time, perhaps ten to twenty years (3-58, 145A). Socio-political analyses have more commonly used data for many cities at one point in time. This cross-sectional approach is obviously more conducive to isolating important sociopolitical configurations than is a focus on a single town over time. Both approaches are useful and complementary; they help explain different aspects, and stages, of policy formulation. We still need to link the two approaches more rigorously than has been the case to date.

The general heading of the sociopolitical approach of course covers many variations. One general persuasian we discussed above as "the economic theory of democracy." It is a general admonition to look at citizen values as influencing leadership and policy outputs; it thus locates variables, but supplies less specific guidance than one might prefer. One problem is that few studies to date have incorporated direct data on both citizen values and policy outputs; most output studies have used surrogates: income, education, ethnicity, home ownership, and similar measures available from census reports. Doubtless values are correlated with these population characteristics; but we have less direct evidence that would be desirable. Let us consider one or two studies along these lines, however, to see what can be accomplished with such data.

One approach to the values of different socio-economic groups that has received much attention is the ethos theory of Edward C. Banfield and James Q. Wilson. In an important paper (4–79) they argued that two value configurations may be distinguished, public and private regardingness, each implying different views of the political process. Public-regarding citizens, often upper-income and Old Yankee groups, commonly considered policy issues for their impact on the entire community. Private-regarding citizens, lower in income, often immigrants from Central or Southern Europe, conceived of politics more directly as conferring specific benefits to distinct subgroups. The concepts summarized nicely many years of work opposing reform government and machine politics, and seemed supported by several referenda results. In other publications, Banfield interpreted English local government as a purer case of public regardingness than the U.S., and Southern Italy as a purer case of private regardingness.

The ethos theory in turn generated a good deal of controversy and several efforts to refute or extend it along different lines. Raymond Wolfinger and J. O.

Field (4–78) argued that the theory might be adequate for certain Eastern cities, but that the immigration experience varied seriously by region of the U.S. Western cities, they held, were settled by persons of varied social origins arriving nearly simultaneously. Hence the ethnic solidarity of the Eastern cities did not have time to develop, and ethnicity was only minimally part of the local political culture. The Western political style was more public regarding. Their basic measures of political culture, however, were reform government characteristics (city manager, nonpartisanship, etc.); these they correlated with community characteristics, especially percentage of foreign stock. Reform characteristics and percent foreign stock were negatively related in their national sample of cities; but the relationship was seriously attenuated within specific regions.

Robert Lineberry and Edmund Fowler (3–15) took issue with the Wolfinger-Field contribution, arguing that region was too vague a concept, and that if a relationship held by region, it should also hold for individual cities. They hypothesized that citizen values concerning public policies were generally related to census measures (income, education, etc.), and thus correlated twelve such measures with city government expenditures (again for a national sample of American cities). Their innovation was to consider the intervening effect of reform government characteristics on the relationship between citizen values and policy outputs. Hypothesizing that reform characteristics protect and insulate the city council from public pressures, they compared the relation between twelve population characteristics and expenditure levels for cities with and without reform characteristics. And, as hypothesized, they found the relation weaker for cities with reform characteristics. Reform cities thus seem less responsive to citizen demands.

Few other studies have found the interaction effect of Lineberry and Fowler, but many have been concerned with some aspect of citizen access to public officials, and the way in which varying degrees of centralization affect policy outputs. Michael Aiken and Robert Alford reviewed five explanations of policy outputs, examined against data for some six hundred American cities on urban renewal, public housing units constructed, and antipoverty program expenditures (3–171, 172; 4–1). Finding little support for the five explanations, they suggested that a crucial variable is the presence of linkages, or interfaces, joining various centers of power such as community action agencies, welfare councils, etc. The presence of numerous strong agencies of this sort in distinct issue areas, they argue, should increase outputs for certain programs. A related idea about interorganizational relations led Herman Turk (4–77) to determine whether or not a general coordinating agency for community programs existed in different American cities. He then correlated the presence of such an agency with antipoverty program expenditures, and found a definite positive relationship when controlling for several other characteristics. In an ambitious study comparing American and Canadian cities, Lineberry and Fowler (4–38) hypothesized, among other relationships, that higher participation by citizens in elections would increase spending, but the relationship was not significant for either country. Downes and Friedman (4–36) offer analogous hypotheses about access of citizens to budget makers, without supporting evidence. (Several other chapters in 3–73 bear on these issues.) Crain and his associates (3–163) found that schools were desegrated more rapidly and with less controversy where school board members were named by or were reasonably subordinate to the mayor. Crain, Katz, and Rosenthal (4–29) presented an analogous interpretation of their findings concerning fluoridation of water in different cities. Many of these studies built on the idea developed, among others, by Banfield in *Political Influence*: political fragmentation often prevents the creation of coalitions necessary for new programs; correspondingly, greater centralization, as provided by the political machine in Chicago, for example (or, one could reason, functional alternatives like community coordinating agencies) should lead to higher outputs. This was hypothesized in analyzing outputs in the fifty-one-communities study as well, but a definite *positive* relation was found between decentralization, urban renewal expenditures, and governmental budget expenditures (4–25). One could invoke the V. O. Key party competition hypothesis, but this would merely make explicit the conflict with Banfield et al.

These contradictory findings for different policy outputs suggest the need for more powerful theories explicitly distinguishing policy outputs. Several classifications have been suggested (4–46, 76), but one idea seems particularly useful in clarifying these contradictory findings. It is the idea of a public good, adapted from welfare economics into a public-separable continuum along which policy outputs may be classified. Public goods are widely shared by community residents, and limiting access to them is difficult —example: air pollution controls which clean the air for an entire city. Separable goods can be more discretely allocated to specific groups or individuals.

Centralization apparently affects output levels differently according to the type of output. In particular it seems that *centralization encourages public goods, but decentralization generates separable goods* (4–6, 7). This proposition reconciles the findings of Crain et al. concerning school segregation and fluoridation with those of the fifty-one-communities study and certain results of Aiken (1–107, 3–43) which show decentralization increasing output levels for several municipal activities and federal programs. A recent analysis of fourteen different policy outputs for the fifty-one cities provides further support for the centralization-public goods proposition.

Governmental outputs may also be distinguished in terms of the following diagram (see figure 2). Policy outputs in the above studies were often fiscal indicators (e.g., dollars per capita for urban renewal), and occasionally performance indicators (e.g., housing units constructed per capita). Performance indicators register units produced in the issue area. Both types of policy outputs are contrasted with policy impacts, changes in the social system resulting from the policy outputs. For example the number of ill-housed persons may decrease after more units of public housing are built. Criteria for assessing these changes are of several sorts. Citizen preferences fit well in our figure 1, and link with economic theories of democracy. Because of misinformation or infrequent citizen contact with many local policies, among other reasons, other criteria also should be considered. Community leaders' preferences are important for such matters as intergovernmental transfers, where

Figure 2. Policy Outputs and Impacts and Criteria for Their Evaluation.

Criteria for Evaluation

	Citizen Preferences	Community Leader Preferences	Extra-Community Actor Preferences	Professional Criteria	Social Scientific Criteria
I. Policy Outputs	I	II	III	IV	V
(a) Fiscal Indicators					
(b) Performance Indicators					
II. Policy Impacts					

Source: Terry N. Clark, "Community Social Indicators: From Analytical Models to Policy Applications." Paper presented at Conference on Social Indicator Models, Russell Sage Foundation, New York, July 1972.

demands of local representatives need to be met. Extracommunity actors, such as state or federal officials, may have strong and significant preferences about programs where they have a major fiscal involvement. Professional criteria may be especially important in areas like fire or sewerage, for example, where professional norms often set local standards. Finally, social-scientific criteria, such as our public-separable goods distinction, may be used; of course these may overlap with criteria of other groups or remain quite distinct.

Fiscal indicators have been the most commonly analyzed policy outputs to date. Such frequent use demands brief consideration of their strengths and weaknesses. The advantages are: (1) They are based on a *numéraire* constant and comparable across policy categories, and, with corrections, cities, and time. (2) They are cardinal measures, alleviating problems of establishing zero-points and comparable units. (3) Given current weaknesses of performance indicators and policy impacts in most cities of the world, fiscal measures remain, however temporarily, probably the least unsatisfactory general measure of governmental effort in different areas. (4) The fiscal level of governmental activity, at least for certain social groups, is itself a basic ideological concern. Left-right characterizations are hard to apply to mass populations, but such a fiscal dimension is a central component of most such ideologies. (5) Costs of government are important to minimize insofar as a basic goal is to provide citizens with abundant but inexpensive services. Precise information is essential if tradeoffs across categories are to be considered. This argument has been carried to its logical extreme by proponents of **PPBS** (planning programming budgeting systems).

Fiscal indicators, however, also have their disadvantages: (1) Standardization of categories is a constant difficulty. Data derive largely from aggregate figures compiled by different agencies using different procedures, certainly across cities, often within cities. Bookkeeping decisions vary: rates of depreciation, full-time equivalencies, and transfers of services across agencies, for example, are very hard to standardize. Functions assumed by local governments also vary considerably. Some American cities provide welfare and education; others do so partially or not at all as special districts or counties assure these functions. The analysis of only those "common functions" performed by most cities is a general solution to this problem. (2) Costs vary across cities, including the costs of supplying a comparable service level. Here one can attempt to standardize expenditures by using cost measures across cities or over time. (3) Transfer payments from federal and state governments vary across cities, substituting for some local expenditures. How to deal with this problem depends on the goals of the research; allocation terms can be added in regressions, or disposable income terms employed. (4) Last but most fundamental, fiscal indicators are generally less important to citizens and officials than performance levels which are purchased with the fiscal outputs.

The ideal sort of measure for many analytical and policy purposes would be a performance/cost ratio, such as tons of refuse collected per hundred dollars. Such measures would permit comparisons of relative efficiency of service delivery across cities, and isolation of more and less efficient patterns. More sophisticated planning involving tradeoffs across categories would also be possible with such data.

Only very limited performance data are collected by American and most other national governments. Some individual cities do record performances in great detail; but lacking comparable data for other cities, comparisons remain limited. If national governments would take steps to record more performance data at the city level, dramatic analytical progress would be possible, with considerable payoffs for local officials.[3]

The situation regarding policy impacts, however, is even worse. It is often intrinsically more difficult to define and then obtain appropriate impact data. For example, policemen, many citizens believe, work to control crime; but in most American cities time studies show that policemen spend more time performing minor personal services—driving people to the hospital, finding lost dogs, etc. Suboptimization is a continual danger here. Impacts can be defined in at least five of the different cells of figure 2. As work in this area is just underway, we mention only some leading studies to date. These concern attitudes of citizens toward public policies, especially satisfaction with existing local services.

Schuman and Gruenberg completed a major study of attitudes toward police, schools and other public services of white and black citizens in fifteen American cities. They found differences both across cities and between blacks and whites within cities which they sought to explain by the socioeconomic composition of the city and the nature of the services provided (4–67). The impact of the service level on satisfaction was minimal compared to that of the population characteristics. The Urban Observatories program has undertaken an even more ambitious study in each of ten American cities; substantial differences were recorded, but insufficient data on service levels limited the interpretations (4–39). Peter Rossi and his associates (4–66) are analyzing data on citizen satisfaction in conjunction with citizen participation patterns and leaders' attitudes in numerous neighborhoods within a sample of American cities. Their focus on the neighborhood is a useful complement to aggregate city-level studies. Banfield and Wilson also are completing a major study of citizen attitudes in Boston; the first results indicate substantial differences across ethnic and income groups, roughly along the lines of their ethos theory (3–120). A very substantial study of Swedish towns, led by Jürgen Westerstahl, has also collected important data on citizens' and leaders' attitudes (4–71).

We note in concluding this section that substantial efforts are in progress to analyze policy outputs in different national contexts and in cross-national perspective. Robert Fried (4–42, 43, 45) has completed work on Italy, Germany, Switzerland, and Austria, generally considering the effect of party competition on expenditure levels. He and Francine Rabinovitz (4–44) are completing a major effort at synthesizing output data for numerous countries throughout the world. A table largely based on a recent article by Fried also provides a compact summary of many policy output studies (see table 5). It indicates the degree of influence, if any, of politically-related variables on policy outputs of different sorts. Peter Jambrek and Eugen Pusic have analyzed budgetary data for Yugoslavia (4–54, 55, 62). The International

Studies of Values in Politics have compared data on "activeness" in Yugoslavia, India, Poland, and the U.S. (3–138A). Special mention should be made of the first journal in the world devoted largely to research of this sort, *Policy and Politics*, published in Britain. Issues to date have stressed variations in policy outputs across cities. Michael Aiken and his coworkers are analyzing policy outputs in Belgian cities. We are also indebted to Michael Aiken for an impressive inventory of data sources and research in progress in Western Europe; the interested reader is referred to it for many details that cannot be included here (5–1). Further developments in this area are discussed in the next chapter.

Problems which trouble comparisons across cities within single countries are compounded many times in cross-national perspective—mainly those outlined above concerning comparability of data. To this must be added the uncertainty in many instances about the degree to which the local unit actually affects spending within its boundaries. We refer back to the first section and the suggestions of Ostrowski and Teune for dealing with this matter.

Table 5. The Impact of Politics on Performance

Political Variables (Study)	Country	Functions	Any Impact	Independent Impact	Strongest Impact	Predicted Impact
1. *Elite political culture*						
Crain (1968), 3–163	U.S.	desegregation	yes	?	?	yes
2. *Pluralism*						
Clark (1971), 4–25	U.S.	spending	yes	yes	no	no
	U.S.	urban renewal	yes	yes	no	no
Aiken & Alford (1970a), 4–1	U.S.	urban renewal	yes	yes	no	?
Aiken & Alford (1970b), 4–1	U.S.	public housing	yes	yes	some cases	?
Hawley (1963)	U.S.	urban renewal	yes	?	?	yes
Aiken (1970), 3–43	U.S.	various	yes	?	?	no
3. *Citizen participation* (electoral & referenda turnout)						
Aiken & Alford (1970a), 3–172	U.S.	urban renewal	yes	?	?	no
Aiken & Alford	U.S.	public housing	yes	?	?	no

			of 9 functions			
Fowler & Lineberry (1969), 4–38	U.S. & Canada	various	1 out of 4 functions	yes	no	?
Fowler & Lineberry (1972), 4–38	U.S. & Canada	various	1 out of 4 functions	yes	no	?
Fried (1970), 4–45	Austria	various	2/6 functions	?	no	no
	W. Germany	various	3/7 functions	?	1/7 functions	1/7 functions (welfare)
Fried (1971), 4–42	Italy	various fiscal	4/5 fiscal types	?	2/5 types	2/5 types
4. Party system competitiveness						
Alt (1971), 4–15	England	various	slight or none; 2/10 functions	2/10 functions	possible 1/10	mixed
Clark (1971), 1–57	U.S.	19 fiscal and performance indicators	none	none	no	—

Table 5. The Impact of Politics on Performance (continued)

Political Variables (Study)	Country	Functions	Any Impact	Independent Impact	Strongest Impact	Predicted Impact
5. *Leftism of the dominant party*						
Nicholson & Topham (1971), 4–59	England	housing	no	no	no	no
Nicholson & Topham (1972), 4–60	England	housing	no	no	no	no
Davies et al. (1971a), 4–33	England	children's services	yes	?	?	yes
Davies et al. (1971b), 4–34	England	services for the aged	yes	?	?	yes
Boaden & Alford (1969), 4–19	England	education & housing	yes	yes	almost	yes
Boaden (1971), 4–18	England	various	yes	in several cases	no	yes
Alt (1971), 4–15	England	various	yes	yes	some cases	yes
Oliver & Stanyer (1969), 4–61	England	fiscal	some	no	no	yes
Boyle (1966), 4–21	Scotland	education & housing	yes	yes	?	yes
Brand (1971), 4–22	Scotland	fluoridation	no	no	no	—

				instance		
			2/7 functions	2/7	1/7	mixed
Fried (1970), 4–45	W. Germany	various	2/7 functions	2/7	1/7	mixed
Fried (1970), 4–45	Austria	various	3/4 functions	1/4	1/4	mixed
Fried (1970), 4–45	Switzerland	various	no	no	no	no
Fried (in preparation), 4–43	France	fiscal	no	no	no	no
Fried (in preparation), 4–43	Sweden	various	3/11 functions	?	1/11	no
Rabinovitz & Lamare (1970), 4–63	Chile	fiscal	no	no	no	no
Rabinovitz & Lamare (1970), 4–63	Venezuela	fiscal	1/2 functions	1/2	no	yes
Clark (1971, 1973), 4–25, 4–7	U.S.	fiscal & urban renewal	no	no	no	no
6. *Mass political cultures*						
Banfield & Wilson (1964), 4–74	U.S.	bond issues	yes	?	?	yes
Wolfinger & Field (1966), 4–78	U.S.	urban renewal	yes	no	?	no
Lineberry & Fowler (1967), 3–15	U.S.	fiscal	yes	yes	no	no

Table 5. The Impact of Politics on Performance (continued)

Political Variables (Study)	Country	Functions	Any Impact	Independent Impact	Strongest Impact	Predicted Impact
Alford & Scoble (1969), 4–14	U.S.	fluoridation	?	?	?	?
Crain (1967), 4–29	U.S.	fluoridation	no	no	no	no
7. Governmental structure ("reformed vs. unreformed")						
Lineberry & Fowler (1967), 3–15	U.S.	fiscal	yes	?	?	mixed
Wolfinger & Field (1966), 4–78	U.S.	fiscal	yes	no	?	no
Aiken & Alford (1970a), 3–171	U.S.	urban renewal	yes	no	no	no
Aiken & Alford (1970b), 4–1	U.S.	public housing	yes	no	no	no
Clark (1972), 4–26	U.S.	fiscal, non-common functions	yes	yes	yes	?
Clark (1973), 4–7	U.S.	fiscal, common	no	no	no	?

(partisan vs. nonpartisan)						
Fowler & Lineberry (1967), 3–15	U.S.	fiscal	no	no	no	no
Aiken & Alford (1970a), 4–1	U.S.	urban renewal	yes	yes	no	?
Aiken & Alford (1970b), 4–1	U.S.	public housing	yes	no	no	?
9. Interest groups: strength & diversity						
Lineberry & Fowler (1967), 3–15	U.S.	fiscal	yes	mediated through government form	no	no
Zisk (1972), 4–76	U.S.	various	slight	no	no	yes
Crain (1968), 3–163	U.S.	desegregation	no	no	no	—
10. Bureaucratic influence (incl. incrementalism)						
Fried (1970), 4–45	W. Germany	fiscal	yes	?	no	yes
Boaden (1971), 4–18	England	various	no	—	—	—
Nicholson & Topham (1971), 4–59	England	housing	yes	yes	no	yes
Gardiner (1968), 4–48	U.S.	traffic	yes	yes	yes	yes

Table 5. The Impact of Politics on Performance (continued)

Political Variables (Study)	Country	Functions	Any Impact	Independent Impact	Strongest Impact	Predicted Impact
11. *Government form: number of governments per city*						
Adams (1967), 4–13	U.S.	various	1/7 functions	1/7	no	?
12. *National-local linkages: strength and effectiveness*						
Becquart (1973), 4–17	France	various	yes	yes	?	yes

Source: Adapted from Robert C. Fried, "Comparative Urban Performance," in Fred I. Greenstein and Nelson W. Polsby, eds. *Handbook of Political Science* (Reading, Mass.: Addison-Wesley, 1974), vol. 8, chap. 6.

6   The Study of Community Power and Decision Making

The Sociology of Community Power

The early 1960s, as we have mentioned, saw considerable disagreements dividing proponents of pluralism, the reputational approach, the decisional approach, and related matters. Essentially, the Hunterian style came under attack by disciples of Robert Dahl, such as Nelson Polsby and Raymond Wolfinger. Various observers recorded their views on these disagreements, sometimes with detachment, often with passion, such that the ratio of ad hominem remarks to new ideas reached a new high. Such sound and fury led more than one observer to conclude that a sociology-of-knowledge approach was in order. And several studies were undertaken to this end—especially quantitative comparisons of case studies as mentioned above (1–107, 5–15, 18, 19, 24, 26).

Walton's results (5–24) appeared earliest. He used the narrowest definition of the field and included only thirty-nine studies (of sixty-one communities)—those of Hunter, Dahl, Banfield, and their immediate followers. Walton found that sociologists reported more centralized power and decision-making structures than political scientists. But this disciplinary relation disappeared when he controlled for method; then

users of the reputational approach generally reported
more centralization than users of the decisional or
combined approaches. When a broader definition of
the field was applied, however, 166 communities fell
into the sample. In addition to studies by those most
involved in the controversies, case studies by many
sociologists, political scientists, planners and others
were included. Expansion of the sample changed the
results dramatically: no longer were there any relations between discipline and findings or method and
findings (5–15, 18, 19). That is, when researchers
outside the center of controversy were included, the
whole field looked rather different, and less in need
of the sociology of knowledge. Further, neither discipline nor method explained any significant variance
in degree of centralization of power or decision making, while specific community characteristics did:
population size, absentee ownership, reform government, and the other variables shown in table 1. These
results indicating the greater impact of such community characteristics weakened the arguments that it
was the method or discipline of the researcher that
predetermined the results, and strengthened the comparative perspective which held that basic differences
in results largely derived from actual community differences. When the researchers who had analyzed
the case studies comparatively proceeded to the next
step, it was generally to see how well community
characteristics could explain variations in centralization. Still, controls were often introduced for method
and discipline. For example, the relation between
population size and decentralization might be examined separately for sociologists and political scientists; if the relation was essentially similar for both,

the results were reported as indicating no differences
due to discipline.

Professional Organizations Supporting
Community Research

Many professional associations of sociologists, political scientists, geographers, economists, planners, social workers, and others hold panels concerning
community research at their annual meetings, and
publish occasional papers in their official journals.
This is true of many associations in the U.S., Europe,
and throughout the world. More limited in number
are continuing organizations devoted to community
research. Inevitably new ones are created and old
ones abolished, so that any list of them is quickly
outdated. As of 1973, however, one can find special
conferences, panels at professional meetings, news-
letters, and similar activities maintained by at least
the following organizations.

One of the oldest is the Committee for Community
Research and Development of the Society for the
Study of Social Problems. It organizes panels at the
SSSP annual meetings. The chairman (1973) is John
Walton, Department of Sociology, Northwestern Uni-
versity, Evanston, Illinois, 60201, U.S.A.

The American Sociological Association created a
Section on the Community in 1972, which will hold
panels at ASA annual meetings, and possibly under-
take more activities. The chairman (1973) is Roland
Warren, School of Social Work, Brandeis University,
Waltham, Massachusetts 02154, U.S.A.

The American Society for Public Administration
has a Comparative Administration Group, which has
been holding seminars in New York on comparative

urban research. The chairman (1973) is William J. Hanna, C.U.N.Y., Graduate Center, 33 W. 42nd St., New York 10036, U.S.A.

The Council for European Studies has a Committee on Comparative Subnational Policy Outputs which initially has organized a new data archive at the Interuniversity Consortium for Political Research of the University of Michigan. Conferences are planned. Several dozen data sets on Comparative Subnational Policy Outputs are currently being entered into the archive and are available for interested researchers and students. Anyone having a data set which might interest other researchers should consider entering it for more general use. Contact Richard J. Hofferbert, Director, ICPR, University of Michigan, Ann Arbor, Michigan 48104, U.S.A. concerning archival questions. The committee chairman (1973) is Terry Nichols Clark, Department of Sociology, University of Chicago, 1126 E. 59th Street, Chicago, Illinois 60637, U.S.A.

The European Consortium for Political Research has an ambitious program of cross listing data, so that interested researchers can learn of available data for various European countries. ECPR also supports special conferences and is creating a Working Group concerned with community research. The ECPR executive director (1973) is Jean Blondel, Department of Government, University of Essex, Colchester, England.

The International Political Science Association has created a Committee on Comparative Study of Local Government and Politics. It holds special conferences and arranges panels at IPSA Congresses. The chairman (1973) is Jerzy Wiatr, Institute of Philosophy and Sociology, Nowy Swiat 72, Warsaw, Poland.

The International Sociological Association has a Research Committee on Community Research, which holds special conferences, publishes a newsletter, and arranges panels at the ISA congresses. This volume emerged from a project of the ISA Committee. The Committee chairman (1973) is Terry Nichols Clark, Department of Sociology, University of Chicago, 1126 E. 59th Street, Chicago, Illinois 60637, U.S.A.

Two joint undertakings deserve separate mention. William J. Hanna edits a quarterly publication, *Comparative Urban Research*, in conjunction with several of the above organizations. It is probably the best single source for information on current activities in the community area. It includes short articles, announcements of special and official conferences, draft papers, lectures, and similar material of concern to community researchers. Researchers are urged to send announcements of conferences and other activities, in advance if possible, for publication in *CUR*. An individual or a library may subscribe directly by writing to William J. Hanna, editor, C.U.N.Y., Graduate Center, 33 W. 42nd Street, New York, New York 10036, U.S.A. A free subscription to *CUR* is also available by joining the Committee on Community Research of the International Sociological Association.

Compendia of research in progress are occasionally published by these organizations. The most recent was *Research in Progress on the Community*, undertaken jointly by the SSSP Committee on Community

Research and Development and the ISA Committee
on Community Research. It is available from T. N.
Clark, Chicago.

Notes

1. The factor-analytic approach can also be adapted for classifying neighborhoods and other units smaller than municipalities. See Rees (2–14) for an extensive review of work in this area.

A word on terminology. Following the U.S. Census, we designate as a central city normally the largest and most central minicipality of a metropolitan area (Standard Metropolitan Statistical Area in the U.S.); within the SMSA, but outside the central city, are its suburbs. Towns outside SMSA's are called isolated cities. Central cities, suburbs, or isolated cities are all municipalities, legally-separate territorial units with their own governments. Community we generally use interchangeably with municipality.

2. This summary of the work of Stinchcombe, Clark, and Coleman on resources is inevitably brief; the original sources should be consulted for more detail. Still, we must indicate the absence of several matrices which complement those presented. Matrices for application exchanges need to be added to Clark's section, and matrices linking actors and issue areas to power requirements for Stinchcombe and to output resources for Coleman. The similarity of the three analyses is also striking, especially as they were developed essentially independently, again illustrating what Robert Merton has discussed as a multiple discovery.

3. There are exceptions. Guenther Schaefer (SUNY, Binghamton, N.Y.) has called to our attention the situation for Germany. Since the late 1930s, every two years every city over 30,000 has reported fiscal and performance indicators,

81

using some 400 categories. Some data are published, but most remain stored and have never yet been tabulated or analyzed. This goldmine cries for careful prospecting.

References

The works listed below have been selected from Irving P. Leif and Terry Nichols Clark, *Community Power and Decision-Making: Trend Report and Bibliography*, Current Sociology Series (The Hague: Mouton, 1974). For the convenience of the reader who may wish to consult that much more comprehensive bibliography, which includes abstracts, the original entry numbers have been retained.

I *Community Power and Theory*

1–6   Bachrach, Peter; Baratz, Morton. "Two faces of power." *American Political Science Review* 56, December 1962: 947–952.

1–15   Dahl, Robert. "The concept of power." *Behavioral Science* 2, July 1957: 201–215.

1–16   Dahl, Robert. "A critique of the ruling elite model." *American Political Science Review* 52, July 1958: 463–469.

1–36   Lasswell, Harold; Kaplan, Abraham. *Power and Society.* New Haven: Yale University Press, 1950.

1–44   Parsons, Talcott. "On the concept of influence." *Public Opinion Quarterly* 27, Spring 1963: 37–62.

1–45   Parsons, Talcott. "On the concept of political power." *Proceedings of the American Philosophical Society* 107, June 1963: 232–62.

1–46   Parsons, Talcott. "The distribution of power in American society." *World Politics* 10, October 1957: 123–43.

1–56   Browning, Rufus P.; Jacob, Herbert. "Power motivation and the political personality." *Public Opinion Quarterly* 28, Spring 1964: 75–90.

1–57   Clark, Terry N. "An interchange model of community leadership." Paper presented at International Conference on Community Decision-Making, Milan, Italy, July 1969.

1–58   Coleman, James S. *Resources for Social Change.* New York: John Wiley–Interscience, 1971.

1–78   Clark, Terry N. "Structural functionalism, exchange theory, and the new political economy: Institutionalization as a theoretical linkage"; Parsons, Talcott, "Comments on Clark's 'Structural functionalism . . .' "; and Clark, "Institutions and an exchange with Professor Parsons." Special issue on "Perspectives in Political Sociology," *Sociological Inquiry* 42, 1972: 275–311. Also in a volume edited by Andrew Effrat, published by Bobbs–Merrill, Indianapolis, 1973.

1–86   Neenan, William B. *Political Economy of Urban Areas.* Chicago: Markham, 1972.

1–90   Tiebout, Charles M. "A pure theory of local public expenditure." *Journal of Political Economy* 64, October 1956: 416–24.

1–94   Dahl, Robert A. "The city in the future of democracy." *American Political Science Review* 61, December 1967: 953–70.

1–105   Verba, Sidney; Nie, Norman H. *Participation in America.* New York: Harper and Row, 1972.

1–107   Aiken, Michael. "The distribution of community power: Structural and social consequences." In Aiken, Michael; Mott, Paul, eds., *The Structure of Community Power.* New York: Random House, 1970.

1–123   Clark, Terry N. "Community autonomy in the national system: Federalism, localism, and decentralization." In Clark, ed., *Comparative Community Politics.* Beverly Hills: Sage Publications, 1973.

1–124   Clark, Terry N. "On decentralization." *Polity* 2, no. 4, 1970: 508–14.

1–133   Gremion, Pierre. *La structure du pouvoir au niveau départemental.* Paris: Copedith, 1969.

1–155   Moynihan, Daniel Patrick. *Maximum Feasible Misunderstanding.* New York: Free Press, 1969.

1–158   Roig, Charles. "L'évolution de la planification urbaine aux Etats-Unis." *Actualité économique* (Montreal), July-September, October-December 1967, April-June 1968.

1–166   Sundquist, James L. *Making Federalism Work.* Washington, D.C.: Brookings Institution, 1969.

1–169   Walton, John. "Differential patterns of community power structure: An explanation based on interdependence." In Clark, Terry N., ed.,

Community Structure and Decision-Making: Comparative Analyses. San Francisco: Chandler Publishing Company, 1968.

1–174 Worms, Jean-Pierre. *Les institutions régionales et la société regionale.* Paris: Copedith, 1968.

II *The Methodology of Community Power*

2–1   Alford, Robert R. "Critical evaluation of the principles of city classification." In Berry, Brian J. L., ed., *City Classification Handbook.* New York: John Wiley–Interscience, 1972.

2–2   Berry, Brian J. L., ed. *City Classification Handbook: Methods and Applications.* New York: John Wiley–Interscience, 1972.

2–11A Ostrowski, Kryzstoff; Teune, Henry. "Local political systems and general social processes." In Clark, Terry N., ed., *Comparative Community Politics.* Beverly Hills: Sage Publications, 1973.

2–14   Rees, Philip H. "Problems of classifying sub-areas within cities." In Berry, Brian J. L., *City Classification Handbook: Methods and Applications.* New York: John Wiley–Interscience, 1972.

2–16   Rossi, Peter; Crain, Robert L. "The NORC permanent community sample." *Public Opinion Quarterly* 32, Summer 1968: 261–72.

III *Community Studies*

3–1   Aiken, Michael; Mott, Paul, eds. *The Struc-*

ture of Community Power. New York: Random House, 1970.

3–4   Bonjean, Charles M. "The community as research site and object of inquiry." In Bonjean, Charles M.; Clark, Terry N.; Lineberry, Robert L., eds., *Community Politics: A Behavioral Approach.* New York: The Free Press, 1971.

3–15   Lineberry, Robert L.; Fowler, Edmund P. "Reformism and public policies in American cities." *American Political Science Review* 61, September 1967: 701–16.

3–37   Vanecko, James J. "Community mobilization and institutional change: The influence of the Community Action Programs in large cities." *Social Science Quarterly* 50, December 1969: 609–50.

3–38   Warren, Roland L. "Toward a typology of extra-community controls limiting local community autonomy." *Social Forces* 34, May 1956: 339–41.

3–40   Williams, Oliver P. "Life style values and political decentralization in metropolitan areas." In Clark, Terry N., ed., *Community Structure and Decision-Making: Comparative Analyses.* San Francisco: Chandler Publishing Company, 1968.

3–42   Agger, Robert; Goldrich, Daniel; Swanson, Bert. *The Rulers and the Ruled: Political Power and Impotence in American Communities.* New York: John Wiley and Sons, 1964.

3–43   Aiken, Michael. "Community power and

community mobilization." *Annals of the American Academy of Political and Social Science* 385, September 1969: 76–88.

3–47 Banfield, Edward C. *Political Influence: A New Theory of Urban Politics.* New York: The Free Press, 1961.

3–51 Booth, David A. *Metropolitics: The Nashville Consolidation.* East Lansing, Mich.: Institute for Community Development, Michigan State University, 1963.

3–54 Carney, Francis M. "The decentralized politics of Los Angeles." *Annals of the American Academy of Political and Social Science* 353, May 1964: 107–21.

3–58 Crecine, J. Patrick. *Governmental Problem Solving: A Computer Simulation of Municipal Budgeting.* Chicago: Rand McNally, 1969.

3–59 Dahl, Robert. *Who Governs? Democracy and Power in an American City.* New Haven: Yale University Press, 1961.

3–72 Hawkins, Bert. *Nashville Metro.* Nashville: Vanderbilt University Press, 1966.

3–73 Hahn, Harlan, ed. *People and Politics in Urban Society.* Vol. 6 of *Urban Affairs Annual Reviews.* Beverly Hills: Sage Publications, 1972.

3–76 Hunter, Floyd. *Community Power Structure.* Chapel Hill: University of North Carolina Press, 1953.

3–106 Presthus, Robert. *Men at the Top: A Study of Community Power.* New York: Oxford University Press, 1964.

3–120 Wilson, James Q.; Banfield, Edward C. "The ethos theory revisited." *American Political Science Review* 65, no. 4, 1971: 1048–62.

3–122 Vidich, Arthur J.; Bensman, Joseph. *Small Town in Mass Society*. Princeton: Princeton University Press, 1958.

3–127 Williams, Oliver, and others. *Suburban Differences and Metropolitan Policies: A Philadelphian Story*. Philadelphia: University of Pennsylvania Press, 1965.

3–138A International Studies of Values in Politics. *Values and the Active Community*. New York: The Free Press, 1971.

3–144 Kuroda, Yasumasa. "Political role attributions and dynamics in a Japanese community." *Public Opinion Quarterly* 29, no. 4, Winter 1965–66: 602–13.

3–145a Meltsner, Arnold J. *The Politics of City Revenue: The Oakland Project*. Berkeley: University of California Press, 1971.

3–159 Wells, Lloyd M. "Social values and political orientations of city managers: A survey report." *Southwestern Social Science Quarterly* 48, December 1967: 443–50.

3–163 Crain, Robert L., and others. *The Politics of School Desegregation: Comparative Case Studies of Community Structure and Policy-Making*. Chicago: Aldine Publishing Company, 1968.

3–171 Aiken, Michael; Alford, Robert. "Community structure and innovation: The case of public housing." *American Political Science Review* 64, September 1970: 843–64.

3–172 Aiken, Michael; Alford, Robert. "Community structure and innovation: The case of urban renewal." *American Sociological Review* 33, August 1970: 650–64.

IV *Comparative Community Studies*

4–1   Aiken, Michael; Alford, Robert R. "Comparative urban research and community decision-making." *The New Atlantis* 1, Winter 1970: 85–110.

4–3   Bassand, Michel. *Urbanisation et pouvoir politique.* (In press.)

4–4   Clark, Terry N., ed. *Community Structure and Decision-Making: Comparative Analyses.* New York: Intext–Chandler Publishing Company, 1968.

4–6   Clark, Terry N. "The structure of community influence." In Hahn, Harlan, ed., *People and Politics in Urban Society.* Beverly Hills: Sage Publications, 1972.

4–7   Clark, Terry N. "Citizen values, power, and policy outputs: A model of community decision-making." *Journal of Comparative Administration* 4, February 1973: 385–427.

4–10   Kesselman, Mark; Rosenthal, Donald B. "Local power and comparative politics: Notes toward the study of comparative local politics." Paper presented at annual meeting of the American Political Science Association, Washington, D.C., September 1972. Revised version in Hawley, Willis D., and Wirt, Frederick M., eds., *The Search for Community*

Power. 2d ed. Englewood Cliffs: Prentice–Hall, 1974.

4–13   Adams, Robert F. "On the variations in the consumption of public services." In Brazer, Harvey E., ed., *Essays in State and Local Finance*. Ann Arbor: Institute of Public Administration, University of Michigan, 1967.

4–14   Alford, Robert; Scoble, Harry. *Bureaucracy and Participation: Political Cultures in Four Wisconsin Cities*. Chicago: Rand McNally and Company, 1969.

4–15   Alt, James E. "Social and political correlates of county borough expenditures." *British Journal of Political Science*, January 1971: 49–62.

4–17   Becquart, Jeanne. "Le pouvoir local en France." Paris: Centre de Sociologie des Organisations, 1973.

4–18   Boaden, Noel T. *Urban Policy-Making: Influence on County Boroughs in England and Wales*. Cambridge: At the University Press, 1971.

4–19   Boaden, Noel T.; Alford, Robert R. "Sources of diversity in English local government." *Public Administration* (London) 47, 1969: 203–23.

4–21   Boyle, Lawrence. *Equalisation and the Future of Local Government Finance*. Edinburgh: Oliver and Boyd, 1966.

4–22   Brand, J. A. "The politics of fluoridation: A community conflict." *Political Studies* 19, 1971: 430–39.

4–23   Brazer, Harvey E. *City Expenditures in the United States.* New York: National Bureau of Economic Research, 1959.

4–25   Clark, Terry N. "Community structure, decision-making, budget expenditures and urban renewal in 51 American communities." *American Sociological Review* 33, August 1968: 576–93. Revised version in Bonjean, Charles M.; Clark, Terry N.; Lineberry, Robert L., eds. *Community Politics.* New York: The Free Press, 1971. Reprinted with revisions in French translation in *Aménagement du territoire et développement régional.* Grenoble: Institut d'Etudes Politiques, 1970.

4–26   Clark, Terry N. "Urban typologies and political outputs: Causal models using discrete variables and orthogonal factors, or precise distortion versus model muddling. In Berry, Brian J. L., *Classification of Cities: New Methods and Evolving Uses.* New York: Wiley Series in Urban Research, 1972.

4–29   Crain, Robert L.; Katz, Elihu; Rosenthal, Donald B. *The Politics of Community Conflict: The Fluoridation Decision.* Indianapolis: Bobbs–Merrill Company, 1967.

4–33   Davies, Bleddyn, and others. *Variations in Children's Services.* London: Bell, 1971.

4–34   Davies, Bleddyn, and others. *Variations in the Services for the Aged.* London: Bell, 1971.

4–36   Downes, Brian T.; Friedman, Lewis. "Local level decision-making and public policy outcomes: A theoretical perspective." In Hahn, Harlan H., ed., *People and Politics in Urban*

Society. Vol. 6 of *Urban Affairs Annual Reviews.* Beverly Hills: Sage Publications, 1972.

4–37   Fabricant, Solomon. *The Trend of Governmental Activity in the United States since 1900.* New York: National Bureau of Economic Research, 1952.

4–38   Fowler, Edmund P.; Lineberry, Robert L. "The comparative analysis of urban policy: Canada and the U.S." In Hahn, Harlan, ed., *People and Politics in Urban Society.* Vol. 6 of *Urban Affairs Annual Reviews.* Beverly Hills: Sage Publications, 1972.

4–39   Fowler, Jack. Unpublished report on Urban Observatories study of citizen attitudes toward local public services. Cambridge: Harvard–M.I.T. Joint Center for Urban Studies, 1973.

4–42   Fried, Robert C. Studies in preparation on local outputs in Sweden and France. Departments of Political Science, University of California, Los Angeles, 1973.

4–44   Fried, Robert C; Rabinovitz, Francine. *Comparative Urban Performance.* Englewood Cliffs: Prentice–Hall (in press).

4–45   Fried, Robert C. "Politics, economics, and federalism: Aspects of urban government in Mittel-Europa." In Clark, Terry N., ed., *Comparative Community Politics.* Beverly Hills: Sage Publications, 1973.

4–46   Froman, Lewis A., Jr. "An analysis of public policies in cities." *Journal of Politics* 29, February 1967: 94–108.

4–48   Gardiner, John A. "Police enforcement of traffic laws: A comparative analysis." In Wilson, James Q., ed., *City Politics and Public Policy*. New York: John Wiley, 1968.

4–49   Giarda, Pietro. "Un analisi statistica sui determinanti delle spese degli enti locali." [Statistical analysis of the determinants of local spending.] In Cosciani, Cesare, ed., *Studia sulla finanza locale*. Milan: Giuffrè, 1967.

4–50   Hawley, Amos H. "Metropolitan population and municipal government expenditures." *Journal of Social Issues* 7, 1951.

4–51   Jacob, Philip E. "Leaders' values and the dynamics of community integration: A four-nation comparative study." In Bonjean, Charles M.; Clark, Terry N.; Lineberry, Robert L., eds. *Community Politics: A Behavioral Approach*. New York: The Free Press, 1971.

4–52   Jacob, Philip E. "Projekt porownawczych badan nad wartosciami i decyzjami ludzi wladzy lokalnej." [A Comparative research project concerning values and decisions of local leaders.] *Studia socjologiczno polityczne* 23, 1967: 143–58.

4–53   Jacob, Philip E.; Teune, Henry; Watts, Thomas. "Values, leadership and development: A four nation study." *Social Science Information* 7, April 1968: 49–92.

4–54   Jambrek, Peter. "Socio-economic development and political change in Yugoslav communes." Unpublished doctoral dissertation, University of Chicago, 1971.

4–55   Jambrek, Peter. "Socio-economic change and political development: Decision-making in 16 Yugoslav communes." In Clark, Terry N., ed., *Comparative Community Politics.* Beverly Hills: Sage Publications, 1973.

4–56   Kasarda, John D. "The impact of suburban population growth on central city service functions." *American Journal of Sociology* 77, May 1973: 1111–24.

4–57   Margolis, Julius. "Metropolitan finance problems: Territories, functions, and growth." In Buchanan, James M., ed., *Public Finances: Needs, Sources and Utilization.* Princeton: Princeton University Press, 1961.

4–59   Nicholson, R. J.; Topham, N. "The determinants of investment in housing by local authorities: An econometric approach." *Journal of the Royal Statistical Society* 134, 1971: 273–303 (discussion: 304–20).

4–60   Nicholson, R. J.; Topham, N. "Investment decisions and the size of local authorities." *Policy and Politics* 1, 1972: 23–24.

4–61   Oliver, F. R.; Stanyer, J. "Some aspects of the financial behavior of county boroughs." *Public Administration,* Summer 1969: 169–84.

4–62   Pusić, Eugen. "Diversity and integration in the Yugoslav commune." In Clark, Terry N., ed., *Comparative Community Politics.* Beverly Hills: Sage Publications, 1973.

4–63   Rabinovitz, Francine F.; Lamare, Judith. "Performance by municipal governments: The cases of Venezuela and Chile." Mimeographed paper. Los Angeles: Department of Political Science, University of California, 1970.

4–64   Roig, Charles; Mingasson, Christian; Ku-
        kawka, Pierre. "Social structure and local
        power structure in urban areas: An analysis
        of 17 French townships." *The New Atlantis*
        1, Winter 1970: 65–84.

4–66   Rossi, Peter H., and others. Unpublished
        volume analyzing citizen satisfaction in Amer-
        ican cities. Baltimore: Johns Hopkins Univer-
        sity, 1972.

4–67   Schuman, Howard; Gruenberg, Barry. "Dis-
        satisfaction with city services: Is race an
        important factor?" In Hahn, Harlan H., ed.,
        People and Politics in Urban Society. Vol. 6
        of *Urban Affairs Annual Reviews*. Beverly
        Hills: Sage Publications, 1972.

4–71   Westerståhl, Jürgen. "Decision-making in 36
        Swedish communes." In Clark, Terry N., ed.,
        Comparative Community Politics. Beverly
        Hills: Sage Publications, 1973.

4–76   Zisk, Betty. "Local interest politics and mu-
        nicipal outputs." In Hahn, Harlan, ed., *People
        and Politics in Urban Society*. Beverly Hills:
        Sage Publications, 1972.

4–77   Turk, Herman. "Interorganizational networks
        in urban society: Initial perspectives and com-
        parative research." *American Sociological
        Review* 35, February 1970: 1–19.

4–78   Wolfinger, Raymond; Field, John Osgood.
        "Political ethos and the structure of city gov-
        ernment." *American Political Science Review*
        60, June 1966: 306–26.

4–79   Wilson, James Q.; Banfield, Edward C. "Pub-
        lic regardingness as a value premise in voting

behavior." *American Political Science Review* 58, December 1964: 876–87.

V *The Study of Community Power and Decision Making*

5–1   Aiken, Michael. "Comparative cross-national research on sub-national units in Western Europe: Problems, data sources, and a proposal." *Journal of Comparative Administration* 4, February 1973: 437–472.

5–14   Wirt, Frederick M., ed. *Future Directions in Community Power Research: A Colloquium.* Berkeley: Institute of Governmental Studies, University of California, 1971.

5–15   Clark, Terry N.; Kornblum, William; Bloom, Harold; Tobias, Susan. "Discipline, method, community structure, and decision-making: The role and limitations of the sociology of knowledge." *American Sociologist* 3, no. 3, August 1968: 214–17.

5–18   Gilbert, Claire W. "Community power and decision-making: A quantitative examination of previous research." In Clark, Terry N., ed., *Community Structure and Decision-Making: Comparative Analyses.* San Francisco: Chandler Publishing Company, 1968.

5–19   Gilbert, Claire W. *Community Power Structure: Propositional Inventory, Tests, and Theory.* Gainesville: University of Florida Press, 1972.

5–24   Walton, John. "Discipline, method and community power: A note on the sociology of knowledge." *American Sociological Review* 31, October 1966: 684–89.

5–26   Walton, John. "A systematic survey of community power research." In Aiken, Michael; Mott, Paul, eds., *The Structure of Community Power*. New York: Random House, 1970.